COMMUNICATING
WITH CHILDREN
AND ADULTS

COMMUNICATING WITH CHILDREN AND ADULTS

Interpersonal Skills
For Those Working
With Babies And Children

Pat Petrie

Edward Arnold

A division of Hodder & Stoughton

LONDON   MELBOURNE   AUCKLAND

© 1989 Pat Petrie

First published in Great Britain in 1989

British Library Cataloguing in Publication Data
Petrie, Pat
   Communicating with children and adults:
   interpersonal skills for those working with babies and children
   1. Interpersonal relationships.
   Communication – Manuals
   I. Title
   302.2

   ISBN 0-340-49457-3

Typeset in Times by 𝍏 Tek Art Ltd.
Printed and bound in Great Britain for Edward Arnold, the
educational, academic and medical publishing division of Hodder
and Stoughton Limited, 41 Bedford Square, London WC1B 3DQ
by The Bath Press and W.H. Ware, Avon.

Contents

For Rosemary Heams and Denise Samari

Acknowledgements

I wish to thank all the people who have contributed to this book: the nursery workers and childminders who have told me about their experiences and let me see them at work; Barbara Tizard for giving me permission to use excerpts from her recordings of children's talk; Jenny Laishley from whose work I drew for guidance about observations by students and Rachel Pinney and Sally Maxwell for letting me observe them doing 'special times'. I must especially acknowledge the National Nursery Examination Board who supported my work developing interpersonal skills training for the Certificate in Post Qualifying Studies. This book is an extension and adaptation of that approach, making it available for a wider group of students and practitioners.

The publishers would like to thank: the staff and children of Tottenham Green Under-fives Centre and Nketewa Day Nursery, Hornsey, for their assistance in allowing the photographs used in this book to be taken there; Collins Publishers for their permission to use material from *Young Children Learning* by Tizard and Hughes (Fontana, 1984); and Barnaby's Picture Library for the photographs reproduced on page 9.

Introduction

Communicating with Children and Adults is a book for nursery workers, a term which covers people who work, or intend to work, with young children in many different settings. These settings include day nurseries, family centres, playgroups, special needs units, schools, hospitals and private homes. It also includes people who work with children in their own homes as childminders. For the sake of brevity I shall use the terms 'nursery worker' and 'nursery' to cover all these possibilities.

The subject of the book is interpersonal communication, that is, communication that takes place between people, when two or more are present. It is not, therefore, about written communication.

A key feature of *Communicating with Children and Adults* is, as the title suggests, that it is about communicating with both adults and children and, in general, it uses the same practical and theoretical framework for both groups. Nursery workers need to be able to communicate effectively with everyone they meet professionally. Their communications with parents and colleagues can affect, indirectly, the children they work with. In the children's interests these adults should be able to communicate, and thus cooperate, as well as they can. Nursery workers' communications with the children themselves can have a more direct effect, one which can either foster or impede the child, intellectually, socially and emotionally. Not least, nursery workers who are themselves skilled communicators can foster the children's own communication skills, which is itself an essential aim in nursery work.

Communicating with Children and Adults shows how nursery workers can take responsibility for their own part in any act of communication and can also help the other person to communicate effectively.

Most of the chapters take an aspect of communication as it applies to adults and to children. The chapters on listening, for example, look at the importance of listening carefully to adults and children; at factors which make communication difficult at whatever age, and how these can be avoided; and how a certain style of listening can encourage communication whether in adults or in children.

Overall the aims of this book are that the reader should:

— become more aware of the central place of interpersonal communication in their work;
— understand how effective interpersonal communication depends on skills which can be acquired;
— have opportunities to practise interpersonal skills and learn to communicate in such a way that the children's needs are best served.

Content of chapters

Chapter 1 is an introduction to the subject, it discusses interpersonal communication and looks at verbal and non-verbal communication. Chapter 2 is about one aspect of non-verbal communication: preverbal communication, that is, communications involving babies. Chapters 3 to 6 are a sequence about listening and responding. Chapter 7 looks at communicating about oneself: self disclosure. Chapter 8 is about questions.

Chapter 9 looks at social control in interpersonal communication, including ways in which some groups of people are given a lower status than others. This chapter covers equal opportunities and includes sexism and racism; it can be taken out of sequence if required.

Chapters 10 and 11 show how to communicate

constructively in situations where there is conflict. They draw on material from Chapters 3 to 6, and can be read directly after these chapters.

Chapter 12 is concerned with confidentiality in nursery work and can be read without having read the earlier chapters. Chapter 13 draws together the main themes of the book.

Exercises

Communicating with Children and Adults contains many exercises, including suggestions for observations and materials for discussion. The discussion material is labelled 'Points to discuss or think about', to suggest that even if the reader is alone, or not taking part in a course, it is worth reflecting on the questions posed. Where the book is read as part of a course the discussion can take place in small groups or it can be for the whole class together.

Sometimes tutors may wish students to use the discussion points as a basis for written work.

Observations

Many chapters contain suggestions for observation exercises. There are notes below for the student about how to carry out observations and tutors can give more detailed guidance as necessary. Quite often it is suggested that the student watches television drama in order to observe different aspects of interpersonal communication. It would also be possible for a class tutor to record short television excerpts for joint observation and discussion.

Making observations

There are many suggestions for observations in this book. Observing is a useful way of learning about behaviour, including how people communicate together.

Carrying out an observation is not the same as just casually watching what is happening: it means watching in such a way that you learn all you can from a situation.

There are two main types of suggestions for observation made in this book: formal and less formal. A formal observation is where you make an arrangement to carry out the observation, for example in a nursery or with a mother and child, and then settle down to carry it out over a set period of time, at the same time making a written record.

Formal observations

If you are observing formally, there are certain steps to be taken in advance. First of all, be very clear about the sort of communication on which you are going to concentrate; before you start, copy out the aim of the observation and the suggestions about what to look out for. Take with you two pens or pencils – in case one fails – writing paper, a clipboard and a watch to time the observation.

It is always essential to obtain permission first to carry out the observation at a convenient time.

Explain to any adults who are present that you are doing an observation as part of your training. Ask if any of the children are going to be removed from the room for any purpose during the observation period. Do not include these children in the observation.

It is sometimes a good idea just to watch for ten minutes before you start to observe properly. During this time if any children approach you and try to get you talking or helping, tell them in a friendly way that today you cannot talk because you are going to be busy writing. They will soon understand and leave you free to observe.

During this time you can make some notes describing the background to the observation; for example, the sort of room you are in, how many children are present, their age range, the number of staff present and whatever activities are going on. This gives a context for your observation.

If the observation is to be of several children, observe each one for several minutes in turn. Do not let your attention wander from one child to another.

Make notes about each episode of communication as it happens, then return to observing.

Devise your own shorthand for your notes in advance. For example, call the child you are observing *X*, and other children who approach the observation child *chA*, *chB*, *chC*, and so on. Identify any adults involved by a number: *ad1*, *ad2*, *ad3*. Use *pl* for play, *gv* for gives, *t* for touches, *sm* for smiles. It is best not to have too many abbreviations as it is easy to forget them. Write down a short list of those you are going to use in advance.

Try to be as factual as you can be in your observation, say what is happening, do not give your opinion about it; so write, 'The baby is crying' not, 'The baby is making a terrible noise'.

This style of carrying out observations can also be used when observing characters on television. You will have to be ready, in this case, to switch attention from one character to another if there is a change of scene, which you will not know of in advance.

If you have the opportunity, carry out observations more than once. This gives you useful practice.

Less formal observations

Some of the suggestions in the book are for less formal observations; for example, the suggestion for observing in a public place like a station or park playground. There may be times when you feel it would be difficult to write down your observations there and then. In such a case you should write notes about what you noticed and anything that you learned as soon as possible after the event. You can write them more fully later.

On other occasions there are suggestions to be on the look-out for certain types of communication as they happen around you, in the nursery or in everyday life. Clearly when these events occur they cannot be recorded in the same way as a formal observation. But it is useful to write a description of what happened and who was involved as soon as possible afterwards. The important thing here is to be alert to how people communicate.

Confidentiality

It is very important that individuals should not be identifiable from anything you write. Therefore do not use any names which will identify the people concerned. This includes children's names, adults' names and the name of any nursery, school or hospital.

More information about how to carry out observations and the uses to which they can be put is given in *Working with Young Children* Second Edition by Jennie Laishley (Edward Arnold, 1987).

1

Interpersonal communication

This first chapter will explain what is meant by interpersonal communication and will introduce you to some of the ways in which people communicate.

Interpersonal communication takes place when people – adults and children – interact. They talk, listen, observe and react to each other, exchanging many sorts of information, in many different ways. It is the very stuff of social life. From babyhood on, we inform other people about ourselves, our needs, feelings and ideas – and the content of our communications is as varied as life itself. Similarly, other people, whether they are children or adults, communicate their experiences to us.

A useful way of thinking about interpersonal communication is as 'messages' – information – which you send out to other people and messages which you receive from them, through seeing, hearing and touching one another. (In this book we are not going to deal with written communications in nursery work, important as these are.) So a toddler who points insistently towards a dog and says, 'daw . . . daw . . .' is sending you a message about something that has caught her attention. She may look towards you to check that you see what she sees. If you receive the message you may give her an answering message – a smile, a nod or some words: 'Yes, it's a dog'.

As a human being, you make use of sophisticated equipment in order to communicate, both to send and to receive information. You use your face, body and voice for sending messages to other people and your senses – sight, hearing and touch – for receiving messages. These are backed up by your brain and, equally importantly, by all your experience of human communication, so that you can make sense of incoming messages and organise and coordinate outgoing ones.

Messages pass from one person to another through touch, sounds, gestures and expressions, as well as words

But this is not the whole story. Remember that any communication is an exchange; there are always at least two people engaged in it. Imagine someone reciting a speech alone in the bathroom or a child smiling in a hiding place where no-one can see her; however inspiring the words or expressive the smile, these two people are not communicating – because no-one is listening to the orator in the bathroom and no-one observes that the child is happy.

In the past a popular saying in nursery work was 'bathe the child with language' (and certainly it is necessary for children to hear language in order to speak and understand), but flooding children with language is not the same as communicating effectively with them. If they do not understand, or do not want to listen, the message you are trying to communicate is blocked. Similarly, there is more to communicating with adults you meet at work than simply telling them something. Unless they take part by listening to you, there is no communication and this is true for communication both with children and adults. Communication takes place when someone sends a message and the other person receives it. Communication is a two-way process.

You play your part in communication by listening to and observing other people when they are communicating with you, as well as by talking to them.

Observation

Spend half an hour observing interpersonal communication in some place where adults and children are together (for example, it could be a nursery, or a park sandpit, or playground). Become aware of who starts any communication between adults and children – the adult or the child?

Notice how many ways people can communicate, other than with words. Do the communications seem to be successful – do people get through to one another – or not?

What discoveries do you make?

Non-verbal communication

After carrying out the observation just outlined, you may have become more aware of the methods children and adults employ for communicating with one another. Verbal communication is important but there are other ways of letting people know what we think and what we feel which are used even more frequently than words. These ways are called non-verbal communication.

People convey messages non-verbally by using:
1. their voices;
2. their faces;
3. their bodies.

1. Voices communicate

The way that people speak has an effect on the meaning of the words they use. Experiment saying the phrase 'Shall we clear the toys up?' to convey different messages to the other person, for example:

> 'I like doing things with you . . .'
> 'I feel bored . . .'
> 'I don't think you heard me the first time . . .'
> 'I'm in a hurry . . .'

You will find that the same words can carry very different meanings according to how someone uses their voice.

Become aware of some of the following when you are listening to people:

— the speed at which they speak: fast, slow, speeding up, slowing down;
— how they pause or hesitate;
— the volume: loud, shouting, moderate, very quiet, whispering, inaudible;
— the pitch of the voice: high, screeching, low, middle register;
— inflection: how the voice rises and falls;
— the emphasis or stress they give to certain words.

Meaningful sounds
People of all ages make wordless sounds to convey messages to other people. These include sighs, squeals, laughs, moans, yawns and cries. You may have noticed that children are less inhibited than adults in using their voices like this!

Being sensitive to voices
A nursery worker who is sensitive to how people use their voices is in touch with a great deal of

information about how people are feeling. For example, you know, just by a change in the quality of her squeals of laughter, that a baby is no longer happily excited with a rough-and-tumble game but is on the verge of becoming anxious. So you quieten the game down and reassure her.

Another example may be talking to a parent who speaks quietly, slowly and hesitantly, using little emphasis. You realise that she may be depressed, and you take this into account in how you respond to her.

Observation

Watch a play or 'soap' on television for a quarter of an hour. Pay particular attention to one main character and how that person uses their voice. Notice the speed, pauses, volume, pitch and inflection with which the person speaks.

What is communicated to other people through the way the actor uses their voice?

2. Faces communicate

Whether we intend it or not, faces can convey a great deal of meaning. Some people control their expressions and look disconcertingly 'dead pan'. Others have very mobile faces, showing fleeting thoughts and emotions clearly. The pictures on page 9 show something of the range of expressions to be seen in nursery work and elsewhere. What do you think the various expressions mean?

Important ways of communicating with the face include gazing, smiling and frowning:

(a) *Smiling* needs no explanation, it is something we have all done from the time we were a few months old and the messages communicated by a smile are for the most part clear: 'I'm happy . . . pleased . . . friendly . . .', these are positive, warm messages. We also recognise the insincere smile that comes from the head rather than the heart, and involves the mouth but – chillingly – not the eyes.

(b) *Gazing* means looking directly into the face of another person, perhaps gazing into their eyes. People use gazes unselfconsciously; for example, you usually look towards someone who is speak-

ing and if you are interested in what they have to say – turning your gaze away may put them off.

In the next chapter we shall see that in interactions with babies their gazing into your eyes and their smiles play a significant part in your communications together.

(c) *Frowning*. If someone draws their brows together in a frown it can show that they are puzzled, anxious or displeased.

Observation

Watch a television play or 'soap' for a quarter of an hour but turn the sound off. Concentrate on how the actors use their faces. How easy is it to follow the story without words?

Do different characters seem to have a different range of expressions? Which facial expressions give the clearest messages?

3. Bodies communicate

Many messages are conveyed by the way we use our bodies; this is known as body language.

Touch

The most direct messages are those conveyed by touch. In different countries people use touch to communicate to varying extents. In Britain, for example, communication through touch – except for the conventional handshake – is usually reserved for people who have a close relationship. Strangers – such as the hairdresser and the doctor – are allowed to touch others for professional reasons, in the course of their work. There are also occasions where touch cannot be avoided, like during the rush hour on crowded public transport. In other cultures, for example among Arab people, touch plays a much bigger part in daily communications.

Even within a society where touch is less common, different people have their own style. Some happily put their arm round a friend's shoulder, or give delighted hugs to communicate their pleasure. Other, less demonstrative people rely more on words.

In your interactions with children touch is an important element of communication. The sheer bodily care of a child, as you change, wash,dress and feed them, requires contact and closeness.

Faces convey much information about how people are feeling

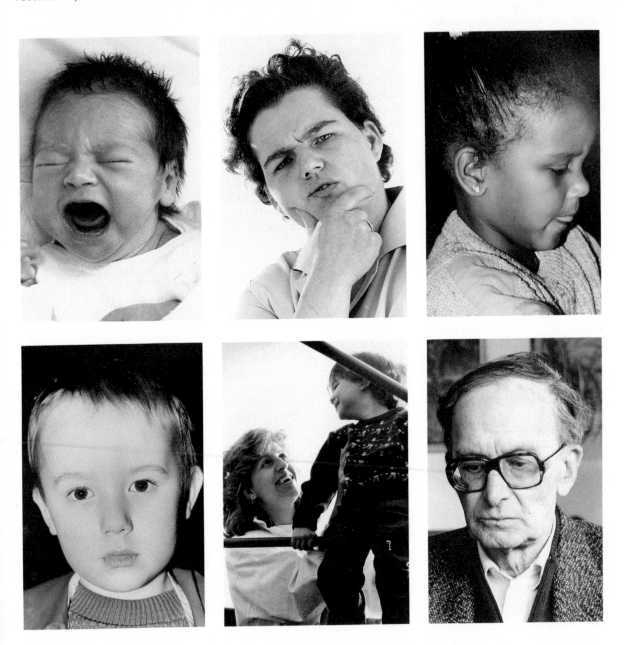

And how you carry out this physical care conveys to the child how you feel about them. What may seem like routine parts of the day for you need not be so for the child. It is not only that these are times for talking as well as looking after a child, the quality of your touch can give many varied messages. Touches can be playful, gentle, firm, careless . . .. Over and above the necessary touches involved in physical care, touch is also important when you play with children, especially with babies and toddlers. Stroking, hugging, cuddling, holding, bouncing and kissing are other ways you can interact with them, telling them in a very direct way that you accept them, feel warm towards them and enjoy their company.

Other 'body language'

As well as through touch, there are at least three more ways in which we can communicate through our bodies.

(a)   *The orientation* of the body. This means the extent to which you face someone or are turned away from them during communication. Orientation includes, for example, being alongside someone, facing them directly, talking to them over your shoulder, and turning your back on them. Your orientation gives its own messages.

Imagine a nursery worker sorting through some equipment on a shelf. A small boy comes up and pulls at his trouser leg. The worker speaks to the child over his shoulder, without turning to face him. This gives the message that the worker is not willing, at that moment, to give full attention to the child.

You can also receive information from other people's orientation towards you. For instance, a new child, who has been given a place in an emergency, without any time for his parents to settle him in, turns away and hangs his head when you approach. You realise that he is still feeling strange and needs tactful attention.

(b)   *How close* you are to someone during communication. In some societies adults usually stand or sit quite close to one another. In others they 'keep their distance', unless they are close friends or relations, and can feel quite threatened if someone else comes too close. But when an adult and a child are communicating, they often come very close when they know one another.

(c)   *Body movements and gestures* can convey meaning. They include such different gestures as waving, fist shaking, fidgeting and tapping the foot. Some of these gestures are conscious – such as waving or pointing – but sometimes people do not realise that their movements give messages. For example, a mother may smile when you say you are sorry for keeping her waiting and say 'It's quite all right, I'm not in a hurry', but give away her true feelings by tapping her foot.

At this point a word of caution is necessary. It is not always easy to interpret non-verbal communication and you always need to take into account other aspects of what is happening before jumping to conclusions about what any particular piece of body language means. For instance, in the last example, if the mother was tapping her foot in time to music on the radio, the movement would have quite a different meaning from a situation where a car was waiting to take her home.

Observation

Spend quarter of an hour in a public place (station, park, shopping centre) and notice ways in which people use their bodies to communicate.

Observe facial expression. Watch their hands and feet. How close are they to each other? Do they touch? What is their orientation to each other (see left hand column)?

What do you learn about the relationships between people from their body language? What feelings do they express?

Point to discuss or think about

Why is knowing about interpersonal communication useful for nursery workers?

Interpersonal communication: key points

- Interpersonal communication takes place when people – adults, children and babies – are together and a 'message' is sent from one person and received by another.
- The message can be about ideas, feelings, facts or a mixture of all of these. A question is also a message.
- There are two main sorts of interpersonal communication: verbal and non-verbal.

- Verbal communication is communication based on words.
- Non-verbal communication is communication, or some part of a communication, which does not make use of words.

- Non-verbal communication includes the way people use their voices, their facial expressions and their bodies in conveying meaning.

2

Preverbal communication

Preverbal communication is the communication that babies are involved in before they can use or understand words. From the beginning, babies seem to be designed to communicate with the people who care for them – they are very sociable beings. This makes your task when you are working with babies much easier. As you carry out routine feeding, changing, bathing and all the rest, it is not difficult to find yourself responding to babies, and leading them into the rich experiences of human communication.

While babies are born with great potential for communication, they need to learn to communicate through their interactions with you and with their other caregivers. An obvious example is that they learn words, and the use of words, because you and other people talk to them.

Their potential for communication increases alongside their growing experience and intellectual development as the years go by. As a nursery worker you can play an important part in their progress in becoming more and more effective as communicators.

What babies lack as communicators

In order to be an effective communicator, a person needs to be in control of their communication and to *intend* to communicate. Young babies do not have *intentions* in the way we usually understand the word; they do not think things over or make plans about what they are going to do or how they are going to do them.

In order to communicate effectively a person needs to have the *necessary means* – like language or gesture – for passing on their intended message. Babies have yet to learn the words and gestures people use to convey meaning.

In order to communicate effectively people must be able to *understand the other person's point of view* so that they can get their message across. Good communicators try to make sure they are properly understood; for example, they speak more distinctly to people with hearing loss and choose simpler words when they talk to children. Because their understanding is very limited it is months before babies realise that other people have a separate existence from themselves. So the ability to see things from another's point of view develops slowly – although there are signs that this is beginning during the second year.

Babies and preverbal communication

From birth babies are already equipped for the experiences which pave the way for communication.

— They find you and other people who look after them fascinating; they are drawn to look at your face and its movements, especially your eyes. They like the sound of the human voice, especially when it is used in the special way that people have for talking to babies (see page 14).
— They have their own ways of drawing you into interacting – talking and playing – with them.
— They soon learn that their actions bring about results, and particularly that they have an effect on other people.

Drawing you in

Some of the characteristics and behaviour of young animals have a predictable effect on adult members of a species and help the species to survive. Think how a mother bird is impelled to pop food into the open beak of a nestling.

Let us look at some examples of non-verbal, in fact preverbal, ways in which babies capture and hold your attention, and respond to stimuli.

Appearance

For many people a baby's appearance – the large eyes and forehead, tiny nose and, later, toddling walk – brings about feelings of tenderness and a wish to protect. It is one of the signals which results in babies being looked after and responded to; it is as though they draw adults into communication with them.

Crying

For newborn babies a significant lesson is that when they cry someone turns up with comfort, food or attention. Babies who are continually left to cry miss out on an important chance to learn.

Looking into your eyes

Your face, and especially your eyes, are fascinating for young babies and they hold your gaze with their own in a way that can be irresistible and leads you on to talk and play. Similarly, when they have had enough of a game or want a few seconds rest from it, you will notice that they turn their eyes away until they are once more ready.

Smiling

At around two months, babies find a new and delightful way of attracting attention and engaging you in interaction – their first real sociable smiles when they look into your eyes. (You may notice even earlier smiles, but these are often in response to sensations in the digestive system, 'windy smiles'.)

Laughter

Some weeks after the first smile comes laughter. A baby's laugh can draw you irresistibly into play – to the great enjoyment of you both. Other signs of pleasure are the wriggles and squeals of delight when you approach and the special moment when a baby first holds out both arms to be lifted up.

Sounds

To start with the baby makes sounds that are rather haphazard. Then at about four or five months, they start to make a cooing 'agoo' and like you to join in, saying the sound back, taking a turn in the conversation. This is a sound that you can get babies of just this age to repeat after you, once they can produce it spontaneously themselves. They also develop a more boisterous selection of sounds: spluttering, blowing raspberries, producing quite earsplitting noises and

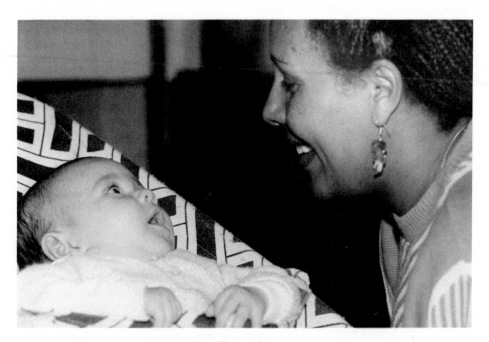

Babies have their own ways of interacting with people

inviting you to join in the fun.

Look out for how they use lips and tongue in small movements, pushing the tongue out between the gums or teeth, bringing the lips together and then breathing out with a little bubble of saliva. These early movements, coordinating breath with the articulation of tongue and lips, are part of the baby's early attempts at producing speech.

Towards seven months, babies produce sounds which are more like those found in adult speech. They produce consonants using the lips – like 'b' – and using the tongue – like 'd'. Also syllables like 'ba' and 'da' make an appearance – all steps along the road to speech, which will develop very rapidly in the next year.

Babble and 'talk'

The babbles develop into repetitions of syllables – ba-ba, da-da-da-da-da – almost endlessly, for the pleasure of hearing the sounds, of the way they feel in their mouths. Babies in most cultures, whatever language is spoken around them, make similar sounds at this stage and make them in the same sequence. But by the time they have gone through this basic sequence, certainly by one year old, they produce the sounds and intonation patterns of the language spoken by the people around them, and spend a lot of time pretending to talk, having conversations with themselves and with anyone else who wants to join in.

These pretend conversations in which you play your part, imitating, pretending to understand and being absorbed in what the baby 'says' are ways of leading the baby further into communication.

Nursery rituals and recognition

Before they reach their first birthday, babies enjoy the games and rituals you build up together and recognise them as they fit into the nursery day. They remember the various signs that things are going to happen: the rattle of pans at dinner time, coats and scarves mean that it is time to go out. They are now sensitive to your facial expressions and can see when you are pleased and when you are cross. Words are also starting to carry meaning. At about eight months they understand 'No' and (may!) respond accordingly. Also, around this age some babies recognise their names and look round when called.

Letting you know how they feel

Towards the end of the first year crying and smiling are still powerful signals, but babies now have other ways of attracting your attention and letting you know what they want. They pull at your trouser leg or at your skirt to get you to notice, and shake their heads vigorously or scuttle off in the opposite direction if they do not want something.

Imitating

By about ten months babies imitate your actions and those of other important adults in their lives. They play peep-bo, clap hands and cooperate in games of pat-a-cake; they remember and use social gestures, waving 'Bye-bye' and blowing kisses.

These are just some of the ways babies respond to you and get you to communicate. But as well as supplying their own part they are continually learning from you. By the time the baby is a year old, interacting with you and with other adults has played a major part in the baby's developing potential as a communicator.

Observation

Spend some time observing a baby interacting with an adult. You might visit a local child welfare clinic, a mothers' or childminders' drop-in centre, a nursery – or arrange to observe a parent and baby at home.

Describe the part played by the baby in each episode of interaction – which may be short or prolonged.

Include the following: does the baby seem to involve the adult in any interactions? How does this happen – what does the baby do? How does the baby respond to the adult? Who seems to finish each interaction, the adult or the baby?

Adults and preverbal communication

If you watch someone who enjoys working with babies you will notice that they behave as though the baby is a fully communicating person and already understands every word that is said! They treat babies as though they are partners in communication and they encourage them to take their turn in 'conversations' and play; they listen to what the baby has to 'say'; they ask plenty of questions such as, 'You like it don't you?', and, 'It's nice and warm, isn't it?', speaking in a special tone of voice, used just for babies, repeating themselves for the baby's benefit, 'Yes it's nice and warm'. They wait for the baby's reply, and if it is not forthcoming they supply it themselves, 'Mm, I like that'. Meanwhile the baby gazes into the adult's face, watching and listening attentively, and taking their turn with movements, smiles and sounds.

Sensitive adults are attentive to all the information they receive from the baby. They time their actions, movements and words so that they synchronise, fit in, with the actions of the baby. For example, during feeds they allow themselves to be paced by the baby; they wait to speak, or to gently rock the baby, during the short intervals when the baby is not actually sucking. They are quiet when the baby starts to feed again. They let the baby set the pace and gently respond to the noises he or she makes as though they are words.

Turn-taking

In this way, from the earliest days, babies are introduced to an important aspect of interpersonal communication – that we take turns, each listening while the other speaks or, in play, waiting while the other plays their part. Later in the book we shall return to turn-taking in adult conversations (see page 41).

Observation

Observe an adult and baby and this time pay special attention to the part played by the adult. How does the adult talk to the baby? Do you notice any 'turn-taking'?

Being sensitive to the baby's 'state'

People who are good at communicating are able to judge from various signals how the other person is feeling, and to take this into account when they are communicating with them. As a nursery worker it is important when you are communicating with babies to be sensitive to their *state of consciousness*. This means how ready the baby is for communication and activity at any particular time. A baby's day has its own rhythm and at different times during the day goes from one state to another. They may pass from being deeply asleep to a state of light sleep and then to wakefulness – fully alert and observant, but quite still. This can lead into activity and movement, which in turn can be followed by fussing and then by crying. They may then return to one of the previous states, including drowsiness and sleep.

A newborn baby spends most of the time asleep. Nevertheless there are many points during the day – often just after a feed – when a baby is quiet and alert, and ready for 'communication'. It is important to take advantage of these times and not just to put the baby straight back to sleep. These are the best times for conversation and play, if only for a few minutes.

As the baby grows, such times become more frequent and longer. When babies are restless it could be that they are tired and will soon sleep. But you may find that you can often bring them to a state of quiet attention – the state in which they are most able to take in what is happening – by talking, stroking or rocking them, or showing them something interesting.

When they are crying, on the other hand, there is so much interference (see page 20) from noise, movement and discomfort that they are not able to attend to anything else. At these times it is better to soothe a baby rather than to attempt any more playful communications.

Observation

Observe a baby, whether with an adult or alone, for ten minutes. Describe the 'state' that they are in and any changes in it. How much movement is there? Observe the arms, legs, trunk, head. What sounds does the baby make?

Is the baby interested in what is happening around them? How absorbed is the baby in any activity – for example, a feed, a game or conversation?

If the baby is asleep how would you describe the sleep? Light, restless, deep? Is anything responsible for bringing about a change from one state to another?

Bilingual babies and children

Nursery workers may work with babies and children who are brought up bilingually. This is the case when the main language of one parent is different from that of the other, or when the child is looked after for part of the day by someone whose language is different from that spoken at home. Children with such bilingual backgrounds tend to acquire their languages more slowly than those who speak only one. However, research shows that they do catch up with other children and later in childhood are at least as advanced in intelligence as others.* They also have the advantage of being fluent in two languages!

Being brought up bilingually is not a handicap, but there is a way of making communication easier for a baby who is exposed to two languages. Whoever is involved in looking after the baby should speak consistently to the child in one language only. So, for example, nursery workers should speak one language consistently, while the parents would always use the other. In this way the baby comes to associate the different languages with the persons who speak them – and is mentally prepared to hear and, later, to use them appropriately.

Points to discuss or think about

'You have to be really skilled to work well with babies.'
'Looking after babies comes naturally.'
'Babies are not as interesting as older children.'

(a)   What do you think of these different points of view?

(b)   What answers would you give, making use of what you have read in this chapter?

Preverbal communication: key points

- Preverbal communication is communication in which one of the people involved has not yet developed language: for example, communication between an adult and a baby.
- Babies have great potential as communicators and can, if you let them, draw you into 'conversation' and play.
- Communication with babies includes talking to them, touching them and playing with them. Communication is very important for babies' well-being and development.
- People who enjoy taking care of babies find themselves talking to them as though they understand. They use a special style of talking which attracts and holds the baby's attention; they time their contributions so that they fit in with those of the baby; they 'take turns' with the baby.
- Babies are most ready for communication when they are wakeful and alert. This is when they are better able to take things in than when they are fussing or sleepy.
- Babies who are brought up bilingually are not, in the long term, disadvantaged as a result. But it is better if whoever is with the baby always uses the same language and does not chop and change.

3

Careful listening

Whether for babies at one end of the age range or adults at the other, interpersonal communication is a two-way process. There is someone who sends a message and someone who receives it – otherwise communication does not take place. So, while talking has its part to play, listening and observing are also essential parts of communication (see footnote on page 16). In other words, it is vital for you to be able to listen carefully, to take in the information other people give you. Think of the occasions when you need to listen, and to listen carefully, in nursery work.

— Parents tell you important information about their children – about sleep patterns, likes and dislikes at mealtimes, worries about the child's health.
— Parents and members of staff speak about changes in a child's family and household arrangements.
— Parents may confide in you about their problems.
— Colleagues pass on details to do with the organisation of work, like changes in shift work.
— Other professional workers may ask you to follow a certain course of action in your work with a child – for example, a speech therapist may want you to help a child who has problems being understood.

Listening is as important as talking

— Last but not least, throughout the day children have so much to tell you about.

All these people need to be listened to carefully for the following reasons.

1. Careful listening means that you cooperate better with parents and with fellow workers because you understand 'messages' that are important for your work.
2. As you listen attentively to what they say, you come to know people better and begin to see things from their point of view – and this is especially important in your work with children. Research shows that children need people who are responsive and sensitive to them.

   Listening to what children say is an excellent way of coming to understand them, of developing your relationship and of encouraging them to communicate with you.
3. When you listen carefully to someone they realise that you are taking them and their experience seriously, that you treat what they have to say with respect.

Exercise: accurate listening

Find a partner and take it in turn to listen carefully to one another. You each have five minutes, more or less, to tell the other why you chose to work with children, about any experience you have had with children and what sort of work you would like to do.

After one person has spoken, the other – the listener – repeats what they can remember. The speaker tells the listener if there is anything left out or inaccurate.

When you have each had a turn as speaker and as listener, share with one another how you found the exercise – for example if you found it hard to listen carefully, or if you thought it was hard to talk.

Listening can be difficult!

While listening is very important in nursery work it is not always easy.

I would like to paint a picture of two imaginary nurseries. The first is something of a dream world and the second a nightmare.

Dream nursery

Here everyone listens carefully. The nursery worker just says, 'Will people please listen for a moment?', and the children stop playing and look towards her, even Amira – who has just managed to get hold of the doctor's stethoscope that she has wanted all morning – becomes attentive; Wayne stops crying about his cut knee; the budgie in her cage stops chirping and swinging on her bell. Everyone is listening.

When parents come in the workers listen carefully to what they have to say; Cheryl, listening to a child's father, doesn't seem to notice two children pulling at her clothes for attention, nor that the twins are attacking one another with playdough.

The parents also listen carefully to the nursery staff, even when they are in a hurry and are worried about getting to work on time.

And the staff are noted for the way they stop what they are doing – changing nappies, explaining how a video works to a four-year-old, adding up the dinner money – in order to pay attention to another worker.

Nightmare nursery

Today is fairly typical, no-one is ever really listening to anyone else. A mother, who looks rather worried, is explaining to a member of staff that her baby has not slept well and is a bit off his food. All the time she is talking, the member of staff is gazing out of the window, wondering if it is warm enough to put out the paddling pool.

The children do not listen to anyone; they all seem to live in little worlds of their own.

The parents are too anxious to listen properly. They think that the staff are critical of them and so they are always on the defensive and do not really take in necessary information the staff give them.

As for staff meetings, these are angry occasions where people talk but do not listen. There are lots of interruptions and voices are often raised. Strangely enough, the louder the voices the less they are heard!

Points to discuss or think about

Both these nurseries are fictitious but they point to one conclusion: listening is not always easy. What reasons can you find for this in the accounts

Shouting doesn't help people to listen

of the two nurseries?

You can probably think of your own examples of circumstances which make listening difficult – whether in the nursery or in everyday life.

Listening and hearing are not the same

It is important to understand that listening and hearing are not the same. While I am writing I am hardly aware of the sounds around me but, when I stop and listen, I can hear a car outside in the street, somewhere a radio is playing and there are voices outside my door.

I could hear these sounds all the time but they were not claiming my attention. I was preoccupied with what I was writing and so was not getting strong messages from outside, almost as though I had taken a telephone off the hook and nothing was getting through.

Something similar can happen in conversation. In certain circumstances, although I can hear the other person perfectly well, what they are saying does not necessarily get through. It is as though the information they wish to pass on is sabotaged in some way. Either it is completely blocked, or something gets missed out or, in some cases, whatever gets through is distorted and muddled. Let me give you some examples of what I mean.

1. A childminder is asking a mother if she could bring in a new supply of disposable nappies. The mother, meanwhile, is watching engrossed as her baby reaches out for a rattle and, for the first time in her life, manages to grasp hold of it successfully. The next day, she does not bring the nappies. Although she *heard* the minder's voice (the sound waves caused her eardrum to vibrate and nerves carried impulses to the brain) she was not listening; the minder's words made no impression on her.

2. A doctor in a special babycare unit is explaining to parents that their baby had some difficulty in breathing during the night and had to be ventilated. She says that the baby is fine now and that this sort of difficulty is to be expected. There is no cause for them to worry unduly. When they go away the parents talk about what the doctor said, but find that they each have a slightly different understanding of the situation. Also, neither of them seems to have heard that the doctor said that the difficulty was to be expected and not a cause for undue worry.

3. A new mother is about to take her turn on a playgroup helpers' rota. She is quite nervous, and worries in case her own child should be 'naughty' or over-demanding. The worker talks to her and says that the best thing for her to do is to give as much attention to her own child as he seems to need and not to bother about anything else. 'Just spoil him today . . . he'll soon find his feet,' she says. But the mother does not seem to take in what the worker says; it doesn't fit her image of being a helper and she continues to feel guilty that she needs to give so much attention to her own

child. As a result neither she nor the child is happy.

4. An inexperienced nursery teacher looks at a child's drawing of two people. 'My nan goes to the hospital with my grandpa,' he says. The teacher is very concerned that the children should start to learn elementary mathematical ideas. 'Oh, yes,' she answers, looking at the picture, 'Which is the bigger one . . . which is the smaller one?' She does not seem to have listened to what could have been an important message from the child.

It is just as necessary to listen carefully to children as it is to listen carefully to adults. Good quality listening shows that you respect them, that you think their experiences, the things they tell you about and the questions they ask, are important to you. It is also a way of encouraging them to communicate, no one likes to be ignored or constantly misunderstood.

Interference

As you can see, people, whether they are children or adults, are not always successful in their communications. The messages do not get through for many reasons – somewhere there is *interference* blocking the way, either completely or only letting some parts of the message through. Interference can come from the speaker (the person who is sending the information) or the listener (the receiver). Sometimes there may be interference in both together! When this happens there is little chance of communication.

Below are some sources of interference, reasons why people cannot receive the verbal messages that are sent to them.

Reasons for interference and how to help

1. Impairment
(a) *Hearing.*   When an adult or a child has some hearing loss, then obviously listening is more difficult for them and you have to be especially careful when you talk to them. The person with hearing impairment needs to see your face and lip movements easily, and you should make an effort to speak more distinctly. For a deaf parent, you should write down any important information. If you work for a local authority there may be a

teacher for the deaf, or another special needs worker, who can give you advice.

(b) *Speech.*   There may be some speech defect or impairment. For example a child may have a cleft palate or a stutter and you will have to be especially patient in order to understand and to respond. In such cases extra professional help is needed and you may find yourself working alongside a speech therapist.

2. Not having the same language
If either you or the other person understand only a few words of the other's language, then a lot can be done just by trying to communicate – going on patiently and carefully, using plenty of gestures until you make sense to one another – and a challenge like this can be fun. On other occasions you may find it necessary to use an interpreter. This could be another parent, or in some areas a local authority adviser could help you to find someone and offer help generally.

3. Children still acquiring language
A young child's language is still immature so that they do not understand adult speech properly and also have difficulties in being understood. As you come to know a child you soon get on to the same wavelength, say things in the way they understand and figure out what they are trying to communicate. Again this needs patience, but it is an essential part of your work and you should spend as much time as you can getting to know new children and helping them to get used to you. Children need people who are sensitive and responsive towards them if they are to get on well and be happy. And you cannot be sensitive towards a child until you can understand their 'messages'.

Even bright children, including over-fives, can have difficulty in understanding you, and vice versa. You have not shared very much experience together and so you can both refer to things which leave the other perplexed, although older children can be very persistent in trying to make sense of what you say. There is also the problem that children's understanding is limited; if you see that they are struggling to understand, you have to make extra efforts and find new ways of explaining.

4. Distractions
Distractions are all the claims on your attention

that can stop you from listening. Here are some:

— discomfort (e.g., a stuffy room used for a staff meeting);
— physical pain (e.g., a headache);
— interruptions (e.g., a parent wants to talk and a child is trying to get your attention at the same time);
— emotions (e.g., anger, anxiety and sadness) that block or distort incoming or outgoing messages;
— thinking about other matters;
— noise.

Avoiding distractions

As a worker you need to be aware of any potential distractions – whether for yourself or other people – and to do what you can to improve situations, so that good communication is possible.

Sometimes you may decide that it is not the right time or place to listen to someone properly. You may need to explain to a fellow member of staff that at the moment things are a bit hectic and could they tell you about the staff party later on.

At other times you may decide that it is very important to listen at that moment and not to put someone off. For example, a mother comes in and she is obviously upset. She asks if she can have a word with you. In this case you explain to the child, who wants you to put her painting on the wall, that you will do so later and give your full attention to the mother. If there is another member of staff present, you may choose to listen to the mother in another, quieter, room.

If you are aware of distractions within yourself, like a headache, or feelings of anxiety, or wanting to think about other things, then you need to remind yourself to listen as carefully as you can.

If, on the other hand, you sense that the other person is distracted in similar ways then you will need to take great care with your communication. You may need to repeat what you have to say and check that they understand. This is especially so if you have to pass on details that could be alarming. For example, if you need to explain to a parent that a child has bumped his head and been taken to hospital for a check-up, you may find that she needs to ask you questions and to be told again what has happened. Sometimes it is helpful to ask, 'Is there anything you would like me to go over about what happened?' and allow the parent enough time to check out what she still needs to know.

Children also need to be undistracted if they are to listen properly. You may be having an interesting conversation with a young child when suddenly the window cleaner appears at the window. If the competition is too strong then it is pointless trying to go on until the child begins to lose interest in what is happening outside and you have answered their questions about it.

You can see if someone else, of whatever age, is paying attention to you. A listening baby is

It's difficult to concentrate in certain situations

quiet, their limbs are still and their eyes hold your gaze in a look of concentration and expectancy. Looking at the other person who is talking, not interrupting or fidgeting, are signs of listening in people of all ages. If these signs are absent you will know that your message is having difficulty in getting through.

What about 'clear speech'?

You may be surprised to have come so far in this book without coming across a statement that it is important to speak clearly in order to communicate well. I hope that by now you understand that this would be an over-simplification. Clear, careful speech is often necessary, but it is not always sufficient for getting your message across.

Someone who speaks clearly does not necessarily get their message across to another person better than someone who does not. If a person speaks totally distinctly, with perfect grammar, there can still be occasions when they fail to communicate. In order to communicate effectively, a person must also take into account factors which are likely to be a source of interference and do what they can to avoid them. You can imagine the effect of talking very clearly about the differences between 'high' and 'low' to a child who is upset and crying. Very probably the child would take nothing in. To take another example, you would be wasting your time giving clear instructions about revised nursery opening hours to someone who understood little English. In neither case would it be sensible to protest, 'But I explained very clearly'. Explaining clearly would not be enough.

There are even times when people do not need to speak clearly, or with good grammar, in order to be understood perfectly. This may be the case between close friends and relatives, people who are very familiar to one another.

People who have a less close relationship need to speak more clearly to one another, in order to be properly understood. In formal situations, like at work, people become more formal in their speech and take more care with what they say and how they say it. Nursery workers should be more careful of their speech at work than would be necessary at home. And, as was suggested earlier, it is often especially important to take much more care in situations where there is likely to be interference (see page 20).

Points to discuss or think about

(a)   In your experience, what is the most common sort of interference in communication?
(b)   Do you think people listen as carefully to children as they do to adults?
(c)   Why should it be important to listen to children?

Observations

1. Become aware of sources of interference in your own listening.

Does your attention wander when someone is talking to you? Make notes of any occasions when this happens as soon as possible after the event and say why you were finding listening difficult.

2. Look out for instances when you feel sure that someone is not really listening – perhaps to you. How do you know? Make notes about what happened.

Careful listening: key points

- In interpersonal communication, listening and observing – receiving messages – are as important as speaking – sending messages.
- Careful listening is essential for a nursery worker: children, parents and colleagues should be listened to carefully.
- Careful listening helps to avoid muddle and to show respect. Listening carefully to children helps you to get to know them and can encourage them to communicate with you.
- Careful listening is not always easy and 'interference' can occur. Interference means that a message is blocked or distorted. Sometimes the interference comes mainly from the person who sends the message; sometimes it comes from the person who receives it.
- Interference can come about as a result of hearing and speech impairments; of not understanding another person's language; of being distracted, for example by discomfort, interruptions or strong emotions.
- When listening or speaking to other people – whether adults or children – nursery workers need to be alert for interference and do what they can to avoid it happening. Effective communication takes place when messages get through without being blocked or distorted.

4

Being an encouraging listener

Watch a nursery worker throughout the course of one day and you will see a variety of ways of taking part in communication including giving advice and explanation, posing questions, asking for help and listening. Chapter 3 showed how listening carefully is important. In this chapter we turn to *encouraging listening*, or how to be the sort of listener who encourages other people, adults and children, to communicate to the best of their ability. Encouraging listeners give other people their full attention and let them know they have their full attention.

Let us look at some encouraging listening in action.

1. Sally is mixing paint when Leroy comes up to her sobbing that his brother has attacked him. She decides that the first priority is to hear him out so she stops what she is doing, gets down to his level, gives him her complete attention and listens to him without interrupting. When he realises that she is really listening, he calms down and his story becomes easier to understand.

2. Renata's mother asks if this is a good time to ask Sally about something. As it happens, this is a convenient moment and Sally takes her out into the garden where it is fairly quiet. At first the mother is hesitant; her story is complicated, involving her ex-husband, how the court has given him access to Renata and problems with his Saturday visits. Sally listens quietly. She occasionally nods her head, smiles her assurance that she is listening and takes her part in the conversation by means of the odd word of encouragement, 'I see' . . . 'Yes' . . . 'Mm'. She asks no questions and offers no advice or explanations. Renata's mother seems to find this enough, for the moment, becomes less hesitant and starts to communicate more clearly. At this point atten-tive, encouraging listening is what she needs most from Sally.

This sort of listening is not easy to start with. You may find that you desperately want to interrupt with a question, or that you would like to give your point of view or offer some advice. All of these may become necessary, but if someone is upset these interruptions may not be helpful in the first instance – in fact, they could have the effect of shutting up the person when they need to talk or of changing the subject to something you want to talk about.

Attentive, encouraging listening can help someone to let what is worrying them come to the surface, while offering advice or asking too many questions could be frustrating.

For example, Michael is worried that his child, Sean, is not eating enough. At the back of his mind is the memory of his younger brother who was always sickly and died in childhood. Sean ate practically no breakfast and Michael feels that he cannot cope.

The nursery worker hardly gives Michael a chance to explain what is on his mind but rushes straight in with reassurances that the child is perfectly healthy, that children eat what they need to eat and that there is no cause to worry. When Michael continues to express his worries the worker starts to ask questions. Is the child having too many snacks between meals?

Michael is put off by the information and questions, answers to the best of his ability and goes away still burdened with an anxiety he needed to share.

The next day he approaches another, more experienced, nursery worker with his worry. This time the worker can see that Michael is very anxious, so she quietly hears him out before she gets round to making some suggestions. He is

Sometimes you need to say very little, just enough to assure the other person that you are listening and that you want them to continue

very relieved that she is obviously *really* listening and he feels able to confide the story of his brother. When she feels that he has said what is on his mind, she reassures him and offers some suggestions. He goes away feeling less anxious and is able to take up the worker's advice.

How to be an encouraging listener

Here are some ways to be a good, encouraging listener.

— Attend carefully to what the other person is saying – you may need to make a conscious effort to ignore distractions.
— Let them know that you are listening, using verbal and non-verbal communication:
    keep your body turned towards them;
    use nods and smiles (where appropriate) to encourage them to continue talking;
    look at them while they are talking – do not let your gaze wander about as though you are thinking about other things:
    use encouraging words and sounds like 'yes', 'I see', 'mm'.

— Wait until they have finished what they have to say – interruptions are often frustrating and may discourage nervous people from speaking. *Don't butt in!*
— Avoid questions (unless there is something you really do not understand), explanations or advice – at any rate for the time being.

On many occasions this sort of listening is more valuable than having a discussion about a problem. You show by your encouragement that you are interested, that the speaker is not boring you and that you are putting their needs first. It's just a case of giving someone space to talk over whatever is on their mind. This helps them to think things through and often they can come up with their own solutions.

Use 'encouraging listening' when it is appropriate

It is essential to become aware of the times when you really need to give your full attention and encouragement to others, adults and children, so that they find it easy to talk. It is especially useful when the other person is very excited or upset and has a great deal they need to say. It can also encourage someone who is shy.

When you try to listen in this sort of way, encouraging the other person to speak rather than making your own contribution, you may at first feel that it is rather artificial. On the other hand, it may seem perfectly natural. The art is in using encouraging listening at the right time. Obviously if the other person is eager to hear your point of view, or asks straightforwardly for advice, it is very frustrating for them if you do not take your part in the conversation.

Points to discuss or think about

(a) What is the most difficult part in being a good listener?
(b) Have you ever thought you would really like someone to listen wholeheartedly to you? Is it easy to find people who are willing to listen?
(c) What sorts of situations come up in nursery work when people need listening to?

Exercise

Find another person with whom to practise encouraging listening. Each think about a situation that presents some problem that you are happy to share – perhaps about a child or some other subject concerned with your work or training. Take turns to tell each other about the problem. Each has five minutes.

Use 'encouraging listening', as described on page 24. At the end of each turn share with one another what the experience has been like. What was it like to be the listener and what was it like to be listened to attentively?

Observations

Become aware of the quality of listening in your place of work, college, home or elsewhere.

1. During the course of a week be on the look-out for any time when someone listens carefully and attentively to another person and the effect this has on the speaker. (The speaker can be either adult or child; so can the listener.) Does this happen frequently?

2. Look out for interruptions when someone is speaking. What happens? How does the speaker react?

3. Practise encouraging listening if an opportunity comes up where you feel it would be helpful. Make notes about what happened, why you thought encouraging listening should be used and how the speaker reacted.

Encouraging listening: key points

- Sometimes in nursery work people – adults and children – just need to be listened to. They do not need questions, advice or opinions. These can come later if necessary.
- Just being listened to can encourage a person to communicate what is on their mind and can sometimes help them to sort out problems for themselves. It can also help them to calm down if they are feeling flustered.
- The main ways to be an encouraging listener are: not to interrupt; to keep the flow of speech going by using encouraging words, sounds and nods; to look at the person while they are talking and not to make your contribution until they have finished what they have to say.

5

Feedback

The psychologists who developed ways of thinking about interpersonal communication and the *social skills* involved based some of their ideas on *practical skills*, like using tools or driving a car. An important concept for understanding practical skills is feedback – information that is fed back to you as a result of your actions, the signs that tell you how you are doing and lead you to adjust your performance as you go along. (See footnote on page 16.)

For example, if you are cutting a channel in a piece of wood you may see that the chisel is cutting too deeply, and feel that the wood is softer than at first you thought. This is feedback about your action and because of it you lighten the pressure of your hand on the handle. To take another example, in the car you look at the speedometer and notice that it is over 70 mph. This information is feedback about how you are driving and, as a result, you take your foot off the accelerator, the car goes slower and the speedometer shows your new speed.

Feedback in communication

The idea of feedback is also used in thinking about interpersonal communication. Here feedback is used to mean all the verbal and non-verbal 'messages' that pass between people in the course of an interaction and have an effect on how and what they communicate to each other.

In interpersonal communication feedback can be either *positive* or *negative*. When you listen in an *encouraging* way (see Chapter 4) you are giving the other person *positive feedback* in the form of encouraging sounds, nods, smiles and words. They are aware of these messages which assure them that you are interested in what they say and that it is all right to go on talking. If you

were to frown, or turn away, the other person would feel you were not interested or were even hostile – you would be giving them negative feedback which would have its own results. They might, for example, stop talking altogether, or they might become aggressive in order to get their message through.

Here are some more examples of feedback:

1. A childminder can see that a child does not understand what she is telling him because he looks puzzled. She finds a different way of explaining to him, using simpler words.

2. A nursery nurse tells a father about a forthcoming visit from the nursery doctor when his child can be examined. As she speaks, she sees from his expression that the father is unnecessarily alarmed. So she reassures him that this is just a routine developmental check-up, available for all the nursery children. The father visibly relaxes.

3. A mother is worried about her child having too much sleep at the nursery. She decides that the Nursery Officer, who is smiling, is not taking her complaint seriously – and raises her voice. The Nursery Officer stops smiling and apologises. The mother starts to speak in a more normal tone of voice.

4. A playgroup worker wants to tell a colleague about an idea she has for organising the book corner in a better way. As she starts she can see from her colleague's reaction that he is interested. The colleague does not interrupt, looks towards her and smiles in agreement. She is encouraged to develop her idea and tell him about it.

Such feedback passes backwards and forwards during all interpersonal communication letting both parties know how their messages are being received. Sometimes people are aware of the feedback they are giving to other people, but sometimes they are less conscious of it. For example, with straightforward verbal feedback like, 'What a good idea' or, 'I don't understand', the speaker is conscious of the message they are sending. With non-verbal feedback (see page 10), such as frowns, smiles, fidgeting, they may be less aware of the 'messages' they are sending out.

Communicating by telephone

Perhaps the main reason why people find answer-phones difficult to talk to is that they give no feedback whatsoever; after the tone you are on your own, talking into thin air! We all expect – and need – feedback in everyday communication. An answerphone cannot support our communication in the way we are used to because it is not a person: talking to an answerphone is not interpersonal communication! Even an ordinary telephone conversation can present problems because the feedback received is so limited compared with face-to-face conversations.

For example, imagine a childminder using the phone to ask a mother if she is going to bring her child in today – it is after the time the child usually comes and the childminder wants to go out shopping. She gets no feedback from the mother's body language or facial expressions. She cannot see her look of dismay, and the despondent shrug of her shoulders so she does not adjust what she says accordingly. If she had been able to observe these signs, she might have asked if there was any problem. As it is she is rather short with the mother and tells her that she cannot wait much longer.

But even on the phone there is some feedback – over and above the verbal communication, the words which are used (see Chapter 2). People use their voices in various ways, both intentionally and otherwise. They pause, hesitate, speak quickly or slowly, they are quiet or loud, sigh, click their tongues, laugh, yawn, let their voices rise to a higher pitch or fall lower. All of these non-verbal communications are feedback that you can pick up on the phone and they affect the way a sensitive listener responds.

Using the phone

- Because phone calls deprive both sides of feedback it is wiser not to use the phone to communicate sensitive material – problems about a child, for example – unless it is absolutely necessary.
- You need to listen even more carefully to what someone is saying on the phone and especially to be alert to *how* they say it.
- Remember that the other person cannot see you either – so you need to express what you have to say very clearly.
- It is useful to be really sure of what you have to say before you make a call. Start by greeting the other person, say who you are and the main thing you are phoning about, for example, 'Hello, this is June Grey from Hillside Nursery. I'm ringing about paying for the minibus we hired last week'.

Exercise

Sit back to back with a partner, so that you cannot see each other, and carry out some of the following phone calls. Take turns to play each part.

1. A nursery nurse rings the local authority supply department to ask why the washing-up liquid and other cleaning materials have not been delivered. They were ordered a month ago. Staff are constantly having to go out to buy cleaning things.

The secretary at the other end thinks that they have received no order. She needs to know when it was sent.

2. A mother rings a school to tell them that her son cannot come in because he has spots. She is waiting for the doctor to come round.

The nursery nurse wants the mother to keep the school informed about what happens and how long he is likely to be away, as soon as the doctor tells her. There is a class trip, next week and they need to be sure of numbers.

Points to discuss or think about

(a) Do you think that nursery workers get feedback in interactions with babies and children as well as with adults?

(b)   Are there differences in the sort of feedback from babies and children?

(c)   Why is it important to be alert to feedback in nursery work?

Observation

Spend 15 minutes watching a television play or 'soap', concentrating on one character in each scene and any feedback they give to other people about their communications.

Do they welcome a communication? Block it? Understand it? How do they give feedback, verbally or non-verbally?

Reflecting back

Reflecting back is a special form of feedback which is useful to have at your command when you need to let someone know that you have heard and understood them.

Reflecting back is when you repeat to the speaker the main thing which they have just said, you are a sort of mirror for them. Although this sounds as though the other person might find it boring, or obvious, you will find that in the right circumstances people welcome reflecting back as a demonstration that you have really heard and understood them. After practice it becomes easy to do it without sounding wooden.

There is no need to repeat everything, just the main points that the other is making and in your own words. Here are some examples:

> FATHER: (*unavoidably late and rather agitated*) I've been trying to get you all day to say I'd be late but I couldn't get through, the phone was always engaged.
> OFFICER-IN-CHARGE: (*reassuringly*) You tried again and again but we were always engaged.

Reflecting back is useful in this case because the officer-in-charge lets the father know that she appreciates that he has tried to cooperate with nursery rules. This is not the only sort of feedback that a worker could give in this situation. How the worker responds depends on her judgement about the best outcome in this incident. For example, in some cases the officer-in-charge might have chosen to confront the father about persistent unpunctuality (we shall look at con-

frontation in Chapter 11). Or, if the father had a lot to say about the reasons for his lateness (say, his wife had been in a car accident) she might have chosen encouraging listening, without reflecting back.

> CHILD: (*new and rather shy, showing a picture*) This is my mum and this is my dad and this is my baby and this is me in my house.
> CHILDMINDER: You've done a picture of all the people who live in your house.

Again this is not the only way of responding. The minder could have asked a question, or made a suggestion or said something about her own family. But reflecting back is reassuring for someone who is shy. It tells children that they have been heard and focuses the conversation on what is interesting him or her at the moment. The minder could move on to other sorts of responses, later.

> MOTHER: He's already had his medicine this morning, but could you give him a spoonful after his other meals?
> NURSERY NURSE: OK – you want me to give him one spoonful after dinner and another after tea?

This is another example of using reflecting back: when someone gives you instructions and you check that you understand properly.

Exercise

Find a partner and take it in turns to talk about:

(a)   last weekend, what you most enjoyed, what you least enjoyed and why; or

(b)   your placement (or work) with children – what you most enjoy, what you least enjoy and why.

Allow each other five minutes to talk. The task of the listener is to reflect back – the talker should make the task easy by stopping frequently to give the listener a chance to reflect back. This may feel artificial (it is!) but it gives you an opportunity to experience and practise reflecting back.

How did you find the experience – as talker and as listener?

Practice

In your placement or at work choose an occasion in conversation with a child to use some reflecting back. How does the child respond?

Use reflecting back in your conversation with an adult when this seems appropriate and notice how this affects your communication together.

Point to discuss or think about

'Communication comes naturally to people, there's no need to think about what you do or say.' What do you think about this point of view?

Reflecting back with children

Reflecting back can also be used when you are playing with children at times when you want to give a child encouragement and companionship and want to follow the child's lead rather than introduce ideas and games of your own.

Children's 'special times'

'Special times' is the name given to one way of reflecting back when you are playing with children. It was developed as therapy for children with special needs, but the approach can also be used in work with 'normal' children, particularly when they need individual attention.*

When 'special times' is used therapeutically, the adult starts by letting the child know that they are to have a 'special time' together when the child can do whatever they wish. The adult will make sure that the child will come to no danger. The adult then pays complete attention to the child, feeding back what ever the child is doing, 'Now you're emptying the box . . . .. You want me to hold the teddy', and so on. Sometimes the feedback is verbal, describing what the child is doing, but it can also be expressed non-verbally with smiles, sounds and actions. The play is directed completely by the child and the adult plays whatever part the child wishes, following

the child's cues. For example, the child hands the adult a tea cup and the adult has an appreciative drink. The adult does not make any suggestion – or attempt – to take the play further unless the child shows that that is what is required.

Children use their 'special times' in different ways. The important thing is that they have the total attention and companionship of the adult for this time.

'Special times' is also used sometimes in ordinary nursery work if children seem to need some extra attention. It is especially useful when you are getting to know a new child, or just for getting to know someone better. More than anything it means being very attentive to the child, taking on their point of view and, for the time being, sharing their interests rather than imposing your own.

Of course it is not always appropriate that your activities together should be directed by the child. There are many occasions when you make the decisions about a child's activities. For example, you decide when it is time for a story or for lunch, or you join in their play with a particular purpose of your own; it could be to do some colour matching, or to work on shapes, or you may want to tell them about something particularly interesting that has happened to you.

Nevertheless, it is useful to be able to communicate with children in this special way, giving them feedback that they are understood and accepted, while at the same time you have the opportunity to understand them better.

Practice

Try to make some opportunities in which you work with a child, reflecting back their play, allowing them to take the lead. What happens?

How difficult is it to allow the child to take the lead in play?

Point to discuss or think about

Do you think there are any advantages and any disadvantages in working in this way, reflecting back children's play, allowing them to take the lead?

Special Times – Listening to Children Philip Carr-Gomme, Rachel Pinney and Meg Robinson (Children's Hours Trust, London, 1985)

'Labelling' as reflecting back

A form of reflecting back is carried out quite unselfconsciously by mothers with their babies and toddlers (and probably by sensitive nursery workers and fathers as well).

Research has shown that mothers often comment on their babies' experiences. For example, a mother notices that her baby's attention is attracted to a bird outside the window and says, 'It's a birdy, isn't it? Yes, a bird having a drink of water'. Or she sees that the baby's attention is attracted to a noise outside and says 'What's that? . . . What can you hear? It's a car, isn't it? . . . Daddy's car'.*

What is happening is that the person close to the baby shares their experience and names it or *labels* it for them. 'You like that, don't you? . . . Mm, that's good,' says the nursery nurse, as the baby guzzles happily, or, 'You're trying to get hold of my hair, aren't you?' as she avoids the baby's grasp.

Labelling is a sort of reflecting back. It is different from pointing things out and then naming them. In fact, it is often difficult to get babies or young toddlers to pay attention to something 'out there' which they have not noticed

*See Rudolph Schaffer's *Mothering* pages 81–82 (Fontana, 1977)

for themselves (for example, they may not follow the direction of your finger if you point towards something).

Because of labelling, repeated on many occasions, babies learn that words match up with experience. For instance, the experience of seeing a dog goes along with the naming of a dog. This is one of the means by which children acquire language.

When you label what a child is seeing, or experiencing through other senses, then you are seeing things from the child's point of view – an essential skill for nursery workers and vital for sensitive communication.

Points to discuss or think about

Can you see any similarities between the labelling that adults carry out when they are interacting with babies and the 'special times' approach described earlier?

Observation

Watch someone, a parent or a nursery worker, feeding a baby (from about eight months) or a toddler, or playing with them. Be on the look out for the adult following the child's lead and

You pick up what the baby notices

labelling what the child is seeing, hearing, feeling or tasting.

Feedback: key points

- In interpersonal communication 'feedback' constantly passes between the people who are communicating.
- Feedback tells you if your message is getting through, as you intended it. In the light of feedback people modify their communication.
- Listening in an encouraging way gives positive feedback, which encourages a speaker to continue.
- Another form of feedback is *reflecting back*.

To reflect back what someone says you repeat back to them, often in your own words, the content of their message to you. This assures them that they are properly understood. Reflecting back can be especially useful if another person is agitated or shy or if you need to check that you have understood their message.

- A special way of playing with children is to feed back to them what they are doing and to follow their lead totally. This is especially useful for getting to know a child better, or for playing with a child who is upset or off colour.
- Related to feedback is when adults 'label' babies' and children's experiences for them, giving a name to what they are experiencing.

6

Reflecting feelings

In all forms of nursery work you are often in close contact with people who are in the grip of strong emotions: a child who is delighted because she can at last ride the trike; a mother in hospital, anxiously waiting for her baby to recover from an anaesthetic; the child upset because his parents have just left him with you for the first time; the mother who is cross because a new coat has gone missing from the nursery. These feelings are often communicated to you and you need to respond sensitively.

What are feelings?

One way of thinking about feelings is as physical sensations and reactions. So if you hear sad news you may feel a 'lump in your throat' – as the muscles tighten. Or when you are very anxious – before an exam or an interview – you may experience your anxiety as an uneasy feeling in your tummy.

Feelings are different from thoughts, although many people mix them up in everyday conversation.

A childminder says, 'I *feel* that children need a well-balanced meal at midday,' when in fact this is what she believes or thinks, which is not the same as what she feels. Or a teacher might say, 'What do you feel we should do – start on the colour table today or leave it 'til next week?'. She is asking for your thoughts, opinions and ideas, not about your emotions.

Although thoughts and feelings are different, there are often connections between them because each can affect the other. So when nursery workers learn that a child is mistreated at home some may feel angry, others depressed. But they do not necessarily act on how they feel; what they think about the situation can have a greater

effect on their actions. A nursery officer may think to herself, 'If I show my feelings while I am talking to the child's mother, it will make things worse. So I'd better calm down and carry on in a way that is best for the child'. When she does this her thoughts are controlling her feelings.

The feelings experienced in nursery work are very varied. They include joy, anger, sadness, affection, friendliness, grief, anger, irritation, trust and worry; and it is useful to be aware of them in other people and in yourself. They can be important messages in their own right; they can also be sources of interference – stopping people from expressing what they want to say or from hearing other people properly (see page 20).

Recognising feelings

Feelings can be expressed verbally and non-verbally. Someone can tell you, 'I feel so happy' when you already know it from the broad smile on their face. Here are some of the ways feelings are expressed without words (non-verbally):

> a little girl skips along the pavement;
> a child reaches up and strokes your face;
> a friend gives another a hug;
> a mother sighs as she lifts a basket of shopping;
> a father frowns when you tell him you need a contribution for the nursery party;
> a child quickly covers her mouth with her hand when the playgroup leader asks, 'Who spilt the orange juice?'.

These are all signs of emotion, which can help you to understand something about the other person's feelings (see 'body language', page 7). But they do not give you a complete understanding of what is happening and you need to be careful to check out before jumping to conclusions. The frowning father may have just remembered that he has forgotten something for his older child to take for a school sale, or that money is short this week, or that his wife is in hospital . . . he may have a thousand and one other reasons for frowning.

Points to discuss or think about

What non-verbal signs would suggest to you that someone is experiencing the following feelings: depression, worry, affection, glee, fear? Remember that emotions can be shown on the face, in movement and posture, vocally and by eye contact (see page 10).

Responding to feelings

When nursery workers notice someone else is experiencing feelings, happy or otherwise, they can respond in different ways. Here are three ways; the first two are not helpful.

1. Ignore the feelings altogether.
For example, a mother brings her child into the classroom, her head is hanging (perhaps she is crying), she takes her child's coat off and hands the nursery nurse his apple without a word. She usually chats. The worker feels embarrassed; she doesn't know what to say so she keeps quiet. The mother is desperate to talk about an upset at home, but does not know how to start. She goes away feeling even worse.

2. Deny the feelings.
For example, it is Saturday morning in the Maternity Unit and Yasmin did not really want to come into work. The person she works with comes in with a bounce in her step and gives her a cheery, 'Hello'. Yasmin replies, 'Oh no, you can't be as cheerful as all that'.

Or the opposite situation: Yasmin is on the way home, feeling really gloomy and her friend says, 'Cheer up, it may never happen!'.

3. Acknowledge the feelings and *reflect them back*.
For example, a childminder is busy with a child, changing his nappy. Her own child comes in from school scowling, slams the door and throws her books down on the table. The minder says, in an accepting tone of voice, 'You look as though something is getting you down. I'll be with you in a minute'.

Acknowledging feelings and reflecting them back can be very helpful. Similarly, if a child comes crying to you with a cut knee, 'You've cut your knee and it hurts badly' is one appropriate response as you start to take action. It reflects back what has happened and what they feel about it – you are letting them know that you understand and accept them. Being accepted is an important experience for children, it helps them to feel secure and confident.

Some people might object that with the crying child it would be better to try to cheer them up or to tell them that it doesn't hurt that much. This would be to deny the child's own feelings. I have noticed that when adults deny that children are upset, they often cry all the louder – as though to convince you. Whereas if you acknowledge and reflect their feelings they are comforted (and often stop crying!).

Partings

Perhaps sad or angry feelings are displayed most frequently when parents first leave their children in the care of a nursery worker. These partings must be handled with sensitivity. If at all possible, there should be a period when children are settled in and get used to new adults, being with a group of children, having a different routine and being in an unfamiliar setting with unfamiliar furniture and toys.

A gradual approach is probably the best for settling in. To start with there should be short visits with one or other parent. Because a parent is present, children feel secure getting to know you and their new surroundings. You can use this time to find out more about the children: their likes and dislikes, the names of important people – and pets – they may refer to, special words they use for going to the toilet, if they have any comfort object, like a teddy or piece of blanket which they turn to in distress – and what they call it.

All of this knowledge will help you to communicate better. When the first parting occurs you will be in a better position to receive the child's messages and to understand their point of view. For their part the child will be in a better position to understand you.

It is important to acknowledge children's feelings and not deny them

During these visits you can start by watching the parent taking care of the child – taking their coat off, taking them to the toilet, helping them to wash their hands. Then gradually you can take over some of these jobs, while the parent is present. In this way children see that their parents trust you.

On the first occasion that a parent goes away, they should leave the child for a few minutes only, letting them know that they will return soon. They can, over a few days, increase the time they are away.

Even when all the necessary steps are taken, some children are still upset when their parents leave. And in other cases an emergency of some sort may mean that they are left without any preparation. When children are upset at parting it is a good idea to acknowledge how they feel as well as to reassure them that their parents will be back later. They may be especially clinging to you during the first days of separation and, as far as possible, allow this and make use of the opportunity to get to know them better. They will gain security as they come to realise that you understand them, accept them – feelings and all – and respond to them. Once they feel secure they will be ready to venture away from you and find interesting games and playmates, in the sure knowledge that you are at hand.

Reflecting adults' feelings

Sensitive communication also involves awareness of adults' feelings and the ability and willingness to reflect them. You may need to show someone – an angry colleague or an upset father – that you know how they feel by reflecting their feelings. So if someone says, 'I'm going to see my mother tonight . . .', and sighs deeply, replying, 'You're not feeling too good about it' communicates that you have picked up an important message about feelings – you are reflecting *feelings* back to the speaker. This is different from reflecting back *content*.

To take the above example again, if someone says, sighing deeply, 'I'm going to see my mother tonight' . . . and you respond cheerfully, 'So you're off to Fulham', as though you have not noticed the sigh, then you are ignoring the *feelings* behind what was said and reflecting only the *content* of the words.

Give positive feedback: accept the fact that the other person feels as they do – even if you think that their feelings are unrealistic. For example, if a mother seems over-anxious about the possibility that her child has got chicken pox it does not help her to say 'You're worried in case he's got chicken pox!', in a tone of complete scorn. You may want to provide some realistic information – perhaps that chicken pox is unpleasant, but not danger-ous, for a five-year-old – but if the mother is extremely anxious you should first show that you understand and accept how she is feeling.

Go carefully, in case you have over-estimated how the other person is feeling. For example, say, 'You look a bit down', rather than, 'You look absolutely devastated'; 'You're worried in case he's got chicken pox', rather than, 'You're feeling terribly anxious about it'.

In some circumstances you may feel that acknowledging someone's feelings could get you into deep water because you would not know how to handle the situation if the other person were to say more – for example, if you think that a mother is trying to confide in you that she thinks her child is being abused. In cases like this, and if you think that the subject is serious for any child who is involved, it is better to let a senior colleague know what is happening and let them deal with the situation.

In summary, if you want to encourage the process of communication, which includes the communication of feelings, try to see things from the other person's point of view, accept their messages and let them know that you accept them. This may not come easily to start with but practice helps.

Points to discuss or think about

(a) Have you ever had the experience of some-one ignoring, or denying, your feelings? Have you noticed this happening to some-one else? What was the reaction?

(b) Are there any problems about acknowledg-ing other people's feelings in nursery work? Are there any disadvantages if you do not acknowledge others' feelings?

Exercise

Practise reflecting back feelings with someone else. Think of some problem you have in your work or to do with training, which you are willing to share with someone else.

Find a partner and take turns to share your problems. When you are the speaker remember to stop to give the other person a chance to reflect back.

Then change over while you listen to your partner. The listener should reflect back feelings and use encouraging listening.

After you have each had a turn, share with each other how you found the experience – being a listener and being listened to.

Practice

If suitable opportunities arise, practise reflecting back feelings in your communications with adults and with children.

What happened: how were the feelings com-municated to you; how did the other person respond? Were you satisfied with how you hand-led things?

Observation

Watch a television play or 'soap' and follow one of the main characters. What feelings does the character communicate? How do other people react to the feelings? Are the feelings accepted . . . reflected back?

Sad events in children's lives

Sooner or later, nursery workers come across children who are upset because of something that happens in their family, perhaps the loss of a parent through illness, death or marriage break-down. Workers find this painful; they are aware that they cannot change things for the child and there is the possibility that they are reminded about sad events from their own past.

As a result, some workers may be tempted to avoid any communication which the child may attempt about what has happened. This is unwise; if children are already feeling sad – or anxious or angry – to deny their feelings by ignoring them or 'brushing them under the carpet' may make children confused and add to their unhappiness. Accepting feelings, and letting children know that you do so, is more helpful. This is not suggesting that you raise painful subjects with children but that if they do so themselves, then you accept their communications.

Sometimes children ask questions about sub-jects like death and illness which you do not know how to deal with. They may make you feel anxious because you are not sure if the children are old enough to understand or to cope with the answer. It is always best to answer these sorts of questions in a straightforward way. If you do not, you run the risk of confusing the children or even of making them afraid, because they suspect the answer must be devastating if it needs to be kept from them. In cases such as these, answer quite simply and truthfully and be ready to answer any further questions that arise (see also pages 43–45).

You may find that you become quite involved in a child's feelings and this can be distressing. If this happens, talking things over with an attentive colleague or friend can be very useful and help you to give the child the acceptance which they need.

Points to discuss or think about

(a)   You are a childminder. A child you have looked after for two years dies. The other children ask about her. Do you reply:
> 'No more questions, just get on with your dinner'; or
> 'Tracy's mum has moved and Tracy won't be coming back any more'; or
> 'Tracy was ill and died'?

Take each answer in turn, what problems do you see arising from each answer? What advantages?
Is there a better answer? What you would say?

(b)   You are a nursery nurse in a school. Gary comes up to you, beaming, and says, 'My dad's coming out of prison this afternoon' (you didn't know he was in prison). Do you reply:
> 'Oh, isn't that lovely'; or
> 'Don't tell stories'; or
> 'Would you like to play in the sand pit now?' (or some equivalent)?

Or do you make some other reply? Why do you make this choice?

Observation

Spend some time observing children, paying especial attention to their feelings. What feelings do you think you observe? How do you recognise them? Do you think that the feelings are accepted, denied or ignored – by adults and by other children?

Reflecting feelings: key points

- Feelings play a large part in interpersonal communication, so be alert for the messages (verbal or non-verbal) that adults and children send you about their feelings. Be observant.
- Feed back that you have picked up the feelings; that is, identify the feelings and reflect them back to the other person. This shows that you accept the other person.
- Do not ignore or deny other people's feelings.
- If a situation seems very serious and you do not feel confident to handle it yourself, let a senior colleague know.
- Answer children's questions about sad or painful subjects as simply and directly as you can.

7

Communications about yourself

So far we have concentrated on feedback and especially on all those encouraging, positive responses you can give to help people to communicate well when they are talking about themselves and their concerns. But there are also times at work when you want to add your own input to a conversation, to talk about yourself and your interests. When you tell another person something about yourself which they did not know before, you are making a disclosure about yourself. It is something you do frequently with your family and friends. You tell them what sort of a day you have had, how you are feeling, what you are looking forward to. You may talk about important things that have happened in the past or about problems you are having at present. It is good to be open, to share experience, and this goes for work as well as home.

Of course you do not share everything with everyone. You can probably remember keeping information to yourself – not because you were being secretive, but because you decided that this was not the appropriate person, or perhaps the appropriate time, for sharing. As nursery workers there are times when you need to make decisions about self-disclosure because, as well as being a normal, helpful aspect of communication with people, sometimes it can stand in the way of what you are trying to achieve. It is up to you to decide when and to whom you make disclosures.

When disclosure is helpful

Here are some points to help you decide if self disclosure is helpful.

Is the information appropriate?
Some personal information is more weighty than other personal information; disclosing it may be inappropriate as the following examples show.

1. A childminder is talking to one of the children she looks after. She says, 'You went to the seaside on Saturday? I went to the seaside too – we went to Southend. There's too much mud there for my liking'.

2. A nursery nurse says to a mother, 'I forgot to take my Valium this morning and everything is getting me down!'.

The childminder's disclosure could be the beginning of an interesting conversation; I leave you to imagine some of the possible consequences of the second, highly unlikely, example! The thing to remember is that the less weighty the disclosure, the less the difficulty about appropriateness.

Disclosure can make for closeness
Telling someone about yourself makes you seem less distant and may help them to share their experience with you. You may feel you need to encourage a shy person and talking about your own experience is one way to do it.

For example, you are a playgroup worker, sitting next to a mother on a playgroup coach trip. The mother is new to the group and seems to be rather shy. One way in which you can help her to feel more at ease is to give her the opportunity to talk about herself. Saying something about yourself like, 'This reminds me of school trips when I was little' could start the ball rolling. Obviously this is not the same as 'hogging the conversation', and you leave space for her to join in.

This also applies to conversations with children. You can foster communication between you by including information about yourself – your experience, feelings and thoughts – and this can be more effective in helping the conversation along than a stream of questions. It can also introduce interesting subjects which stretch children's understanding and widen their horizons.

Points to discuss or think about

(a)   Can you remember interesting adults from your own childhood? What sorts of things did they tell you about? Think of things that got the conversation going – photographs, knick-knacks, treasures. Is there any way that you could use your own personal belongings – things you take out of your pocket or handbag (not nursery equipment) – to start conversations with children? Are there any things you could bring from home?

(b)   In your experience, is it easier to make conversation (not just questions and answers) with children or with adults?

Sharing experience can show understanding

By talking about your own experience it is possible to show that you understand the other person's problem. A teacher says to a mother, 'He's still waking you up during the night? I know what it's like; I had the same with mine. I used to long for six hours' undisturbed sleep'. The mother knows that the teacher appreciates her situation.

Remember, though, that the two experiences may be very different. You may not really understand how another person is experiencing a difficult situation even though you have gone through something that seems similar yourself. For example, the feelings involved in one divorce may be totally unlike those involved in another.

When disclosure is unhelpful

Disclosure can be a burden

Sharing your problems may mean burdening other people with them, fine between friends, but not appropriate where your relationship is a professional one. Your job is to be of service to the children and their families, they have no such obligations towards you.

Similarly, self-disclosure can shift the focus of a conversation to your interests at a point when this may not be useful. If a mother wants to tell you that her baby will not feed, telling her how your young niece is now on solids would be a distraction, suggesting you are not interested in what she has to say. There are many times in your work, as we saw earlier, when encouraging listening and reflecting back are the most useful response.

Friends or friendly?

Some personal statements may suggest that you see yourself as a 'friend', rather than 'friendly'. There is a difference – you choose your friends, but not your professional relationships. Friends have a fairly equal relationship based on liking to be with one another. But relationships with colleagues, parents and children are not personal choices. Sometimes you may even find yourself working with people you do not really like. Working relationships are based on providing a service for children and parents and on cooperating with colleagues – although personal friendships can develop. But behaving differently with different parents, disclosing more about yourself to some than to others, suggests that you prefer them, that you have favourites. This is not to say that 'friendliness' – sensitivity, encouragement, warmth – is out of place, but that to the best of your ability you should show it equally to all parents.

Points to discuss or think about

(a)   Bearing in mind what you have just read, how appropriate would it be for a nursery worker to say the following to a parent?

> 'Monday again, I didn't feel like coming into work this morning.'
> 'I'm going to be away for a couple of weeks because I'm getting married.'
> 'I spent most of the weekend working for the local Labour Party/Conservative Party/Alliance Party.'
> 'I know what you mean, I'm widowed myself.'
> 'I'm at my wit's end about my father. I feel I ought to stay at home to look after him, but I need to work for the money.'
> 'I'm feeling great today!'

Which was the most difficult statement to decide about? Why?

(b)   'You can't make rules about self-disclosure – it depends where you're working: if you're a nanny, a childminder, a nursery officer in a hospital or whatever.' What do you think?

'You can be friends with the parents.' What do you think?

(c) What reasons can you think of for and against nursery workers wearing political badges or religious symbols?

(d) Should you ever talk to parents about difficulties with colleagues?

Observation

Become aware of the part of self-disclosure in people's conversations. Listen in buses, shops, wherever you are. Or watch a play or 'soap' on television and for a quarter of an hour concentrate on one character. Does the character use encouraging listening, reflecting back, questions or disclosure? One more than the other or equally?

Was there anything you noticed about the part that self-disclosure plays in communication?

Communications about yourself: key points

- Self-disclosure is giving other people information about yourself which they would not otherwise know and it can have advantages.
- Self-disclosure can encourage others to make disclosures about themselves, that is, start them talking.
- Self-disclosure can make you seem more approachable.
- Disclosing something about your own experience may suggest that you understand and sympathise with another person's situation. But be careful, this may be misleading.
- Self-disclosure also has disadvantages. It can burden other people with your problems; change the focus from the other person to yourself; suggest that you are a 'friend' rather than 'friendly'; suggest 'favouritism' if you disclose more to some people than to others.

8

Questions

Good interpersonal communication involves many activities: observing and listening, avoiding interference, reflecting back and talking about yourself. This chapter introduces the use of questions in nursery work. Asking questions is a very familiar activity but we are not always aware of the effect that questions, and different sorts of questions, can have in our communications with adults and children – sometimes they help things along but at other times they can get in the way.

Open and closed questions

Asking questions well is an art in itself – think of a good radio interview compared with an amateur attempt. An experienced interviewer just seems to start a conversation going, guiding it along with questions, drawing out the experience of the person being interviewed. Other interviewers just shut the other person up with a stream of questions which get answered in monosyllables. The sort of question used will often have a direct effect on the reply given. A useful way of grouping questions is according to whether they are closed or open.

Closed questions

These are questions which can be answered fairly simply, often with the words 'Yes' or 'No', or where the answer must be short and limited. For example:

> 'Did you enjoy the film?'
> 'You've drawn a house, haven't you?'
> 'Is that a pussy cat?'
> 'Do you like mushrooms?'
> 'Have you heard their new single?'
> 'Would you like the red cup or the blue one?'

If you ask mainly closed questions, someone who is feeling shy (for example, a child, a new parent or new member of staff) may answer with one word and then it is back to you to continue the conversation. Another way of saying this is that when you are asking closed questions you are taking control of the conversation and leaving very little space for the other person to make their contribution and to introduce subjects they are interested in.

Open questions

Open questions give the other person much more choice in how they answer. They often begin with either 'How' or 'Why':

> 'Why did you want to see me?'
> 'How did you get the icing smooth like that?'
> 'How does the new flat compare with where you were before?'
> 'How do you feel about that?'

The person answering is never limited to 'Yes' or 'No' with open questions, they are given the opportunity for longer answers. This does not mean that you should never use closed questions. They are useful for clarification and for obtaining simple information. But open questions are better if you want to encourage the other person to talk about their experience.

'How' questions sometimes feel easier to answer than 'Why' questions. You may notice a difference in feeling between, 'How did you come to send her to nursery?' and, 'Why did you send her to nursery?'. The first is asking a mother to tell something of her experience and the second could, in some circumstances, be interpreted as asking her to justify her action.

Exercise

Twenty questions. Find a partner and each write down the name of a child you know. Each has twenty questions to find out as much as possible about their partner's child – for example, background, development and temperament. The only answers allowed are 'Yes' or 'No' so questions must be framed accordingly – that is they must be closed questions.

Try the exercise again, with a different partner; this time you are both allowed to use open questions.

What differences did you notice between the two exercises – as a questioner and as a speaker? How did you feel? Did open questions or closed questions give you a better picture of the child?

Helpful questions

Questions can make space for others to talk

Mothers and other caregivers constantly use questions as a way of showing that babies can take their turn in a 'conversation'. 'You like that, don't you?' the mother says to her two-month-old baby, long before there is any chance of the baby responding. Short questions of this sort, tagged on to the end of statements, are often used to indicate to others that it is their turn to join in a conversation. They are called 'tag' questions. 'It was a good film, wasn't it?' you ask or, after giving your opinion, you hand the topic over with a question like, 'You know what I mean?'.

Sometimes questions are used to reflect back. Someone says, 'I really like working in the Special Baby Unit' and her friend answers with a question which reflects back what has just been said, 'You're enjoying it then?', at which the first speaker carries on about her experience. Or a nursery worker can use a short question just to keep a child talking. 'I went out with my mummy,' says the child. 'Did you?' asks the worker, showing interest. 'Yes, and we saw daddy's nannie,' continues the child, encouraged by the question.

Questions can make things clear

Sometimes you need to ask questions to clarify a situation, something is not clear, you do not understand or you need extra information. Occasionally people are diffident about this and are afraid to ask about something in case they look

foolish. This is a mistake which can lead to difficulties and confusion.

For example, a new member of staff on a maternity ward is told that a baby is going to have a Guthrie test. She does not know what this is but feels too shy to ask. Later, when she is helping the mother feed the baby, the mother seems to be upset; she asks about the test and if it means that something is wrong with the baby. The nursery nurse's hesitation does not help the situation. Because she does not know she cannot reply that the test is routine. Her embarrassment gives the impression that there is something she does not want to talk about.

Questions show you are interested

Questions can also show that you have a friendly interest in someone; they help the other person to relax and talk more easily about themselves. 'Where did you go for your holiday? What was it like?' may start the ball rolling.

When questions are unhelpful

Too many questions

Although asking questions can show that you are interested in the other person, asking too many questions can be daunting, almost inquisitorial. So you need to be ready to use other communication skills if a conversation is getting stuck. You can say something about your own experience, like, 'I can never manage the icing properly so I get my friend to do it for me', followed by another question if necessary: 'How did you learn to do it?'. Or you can use reflecting back, 'It's for Joni's birthday?', and wait for an answer.

Sensitive questions

We have all, at sometime or other, met people who ask questions about things which are none of their business, questions which touch on sensitive areas and which give rise to resentment. In most nursery work questions about another person's private life are not necessary and so these sorts of questions should not arise. But sometimes senior workers need to ask sensitive questions in order to clarify a situation.

For example, it may seem from something a father has just said that a child's mother has left home. A childminder worker may decide to clarify this with a question: ' I don't know if I got

WHAT COLOUR.....
HOW MANY....?????

Too many questions can put an end to communication

it right, but is Emma's mother not living with you and Emma now?'. Clearly if the father had wished to convey this information, then it is important for the nursery worker to know such details and the question was justifiable.

Nevertheless, such questions can be threatening and intrusive. Before asking sensitive questions decide:

'Is it essential for me to find out about this? Do I really need to know for the good of the child and in order to carry out my professional duties?'

'Am I the right person to be asking this question? Perhaps it would be better to talk to a senior worker about any anxiety I have about the child's welfare.'

Asking questions carries responsibilities

Encouraging self-disclosure (see Chapter 7) in any way, including by asking questions, carries the responsibility for using the information for the good of the child. If, to take an extreme example, as a result of your questions a mother confides that her boyfriend is abusing a child, then it is your responsibility to pass the information on. This may be to your officer-in-charge, ward sister or head teacher. If you yourself are in charge, or are working as a salaried childminder, you should talk to your line manager. You must also tell the mother that you are going to pass the information on (see page 63).

Points to discuss or think about

Two childminders are talking at their local drop-in centre. One says to the other, 'I'd never ask parents questions about their private lives, no matter what I thought was happening'. The other replies, 'Well, I think I would if I had to. But with children it's difficult. You should never ask children questions about their families.'

What would you say if you joined in the conversation? What reasons would you give?

Observations

1. Become aware of the part questions play in interpersonal communication in everyday life. Do questions seem to help a conversation along or put a stop to it?

2. Watch some interviews on television, or listen to interviews on the radio. Does the interviewer use open or closed questions? Are there any questions which seem to threaten the interviewee? Do you notice any differences between interviewers?

Asking children questions

Asking questions has been one of the methods used in education for thousands of years. As we have seen, some questions are encouraging and help children to communicate. Careful questions can lead pupils to make discoveries for themselves and draw their attention to different aspects of a problem.

Another reason for asking questions is to find out what a child knows; for example questions about colour, number or size. But asking children certain sorts of questions can become a habit without any real purpose, for example, 'What a nice house. What colour is it?'. Stock questions like this may be no more than paying the child a bit of verbal attention in passing, especially if you do not really need to test the child's knowledge of colour.

Researchers have found that when nursery staff use questions a lot in conversations with children, the children seem to clam up or answer only in monosyllables.* Closed questions especially can have this effect. Also, sometimes the worker concerned hardly seems to listen to the answer given, but just goes straight on to another question.

On the other hand, reflecting back or labelling (see pages 29 and 30), gives children information, shows that you are taking in what they are doing and encourages them to speak. For example, saying something like, 'You've painted it all green, except for this bit here, haven't you?' keeps the conversation focused on the child's own activities and leaves space for their contribution to the conversation. And, as always, you can disclose something about yourself to help the conversation along if you wish.

Notice how the child (or children) respond to questions. Do they seem to help the child take part in the conversation?

Children's questions

Children can be persistent questioners when they really need information for their own purposes and especially when they are puzzled – when something does not make sense according to their present understanding of the world. One researcher calls this sort of questioning *intellectual search*. Children can be interested in many different fields of knowledge, such as the economic system, zoology or the child's own personal history – anything which has come to their notice

* See *Working with Under-Fives* David Wood et al (Grant McIntyre, 1980) and *Young Children Learning* Barbara Tizard and Martin Hughes (Fontana, 1984)

and arouses their curiosity.

These persistent questions can often be difficult for nursery workers, whether because they do not know the answers to questions like, 'Why doesn't the fly fall off the ceiling?' or because they cannot see things from the child's point of view – they do not fully understand the background of information and knowledge a child already has. Often they may not know enough about children's lives outside the nursery to make sense of what children say. In these circumstances it is worth being patient, and asking questions to discover what they mean. Trying to understand a child's point of view and then providing the information they require is a useful piece of interpersonal communication. In this way children find out about the world, expand their knowledge and put right their misunderstandings.

Exercise

Read the following conversation (which was recorded in real life) and pay special attention to the child's questions.

The conversation takes place at home between a mother and a three-year-old girl. A neighbour, Pamela, has just left.

GIRL: What did Pamela say?

MOTHER: She's having to pay everybody else's bills for the window-cleaner 'cause they're all out.

GIRL: Why are they all out?

MOTHER: 'Cause they're working or something.

GIRL: Aren't they silly?

MOTHER: Well, you have to work to earn money, don't you?

GIRL: Yeah, if they know what day the window-cleaner comes, they should stay here.

MOTHER: They should stay at home? Well, I don't know, they can't always . . .

(*At this point there is a change in the conversation, but the girl raises the subject again, later.*)

GIRL: Mummy?

MOTHER: Mmm.

GIRL: Umm . . . she can't pay everybody's, er . . . all the bills to the window-cleaner can she?

MOTHER: No she can't pay everybody's bills . . . she sometimes pays mine if I'm out.

GIRL: 'Cause it's fair.

MOTHER: Mm, it is.

GIRL: Umm, where does she leave the money?

MOTHER: She doesn't leave it anywhere, she hands it to the window-cleaner when he's finished.

GIRL: And then she gives it to us?

MOTHER: No, no she doesn't have to pay us.

GIRL: Then the window-cleaner gives it to us?

MOTHER: No, we give the window-cleaner money, he does work for us, and we have to give him money.

GIRL: Why?

MOTHER: Well, because he's been working for us cleaning our windows. He doesn't do it for nothing.

GIRL: Why do you have money if you have . . . if people clean your windows?

MOTHER: Well, the window-cleaner needs money, doesn't he?

GIRL: Why?

MOTHER: To buy clothes for his children and food for them to eat.

GIRL: Well, sometimes window-cleaners don't have children.

MOTHER: Quite often they do.

GIRL: And something on his own to eat, and for curtains?

MOTHER: And for paying his gas bill and electricity bill and for paying for petrol for his car. All sorts of things you have to pay for, you see. You have to earn money somehow, and he earns it by cleaning other people's windows and big shop windows and things.

GIRL: And the person who got the money gives it to people . . .

(a)   What misunderstandings or puzzlements does the girl have?

(b)   What information does the mother give the girl?

(c)   How useful do you think conversations like these are in developing children's understanding?

Observations

Over the next few weeks, be on the look-out for children's questions: single questions or sequences of questions, when a child is determined to find out more or to get at the root of something. If you are involved, answer patiently without changing the subject.

Describe any sequence of questions that you find interesting.

Say what lies behind the children's questions – what lack of understanding or need for information.

Points to discuss or think about

(a)   Can you remember teachers asking questions when you were at school? How did you feel when you were asked questions?

(b)   What are the disadvantages, in your experience, connected with asking children questions? How do you feel about these questions?

Exercise

Read the following conversation and look carefully at the nursery worker's questions. Do they help the child to communicate? Can you suggest other things that the worker could have said?

A four-year-old boy is looking at a picture of a rabbit looking at a newspaper and telling his friend that it is a mouse.

NURSERY WORKER: It isn't a mouse, actually. Do you know what it is?

BOY: (*no answer*)

NURSERY WORKER: Do you know how they make a warren?

BOY: What's their name?

NURSERY WORKER: They don't have names, they're just rabbits. Does your daddy read newspapers?

BOY: I've got lots of books.

NURSERY WORKER: Does he read them to you?

BOY: Depends.

NURSERY WORKER: What books does he read to you?

BOY: My brother's name is Ian.

NURSERY WORKER: Put the book away when you've finished.

Observation

Observe an adult with a child or a group of children – it could be a nursery worker or a parent and child. A mealtime could be a good time to choose. Notice what part, if any, questions play. What sort of questions are asked: open questions, closed questions, 'tag' questions, (see pages 40 and 41)? Include any difficulties you have in understanding what lies behind the questions – your own puzzlement.

Questions: key points

- In conversations with adults and children, questions can help communications along or they can get in the way.
- Closed questions usually need one-word answers, for example 'Yes' or 'No', and leave very little space for the other person to make a contribution.
- Open questions often begin with 'Why' or 'How', and give the other person much more scope for answering at greater length.
- Some questions, known as 'tag' questions, are not real questions, they are just a way of indicating that you have finished your turn in the conversation. They include phrases like, 'Isn't it?'. Tag questions are used between adults and in conversations with children, including with babies.
- Questions can be used for clarification when you are not sure about something.
- Questions can be used to show that you have a friendly interest in someone.
- Do not ask too many questions or insensitive, tactless questions.
- With children, only ask questions if you really need to know the answer, for example, to carry on your conversation, or if you really need to find out what a child knows.
- Be sparing with questions and if you ask them listen to the answers.
- Children can ask questions persistently when they are in search of knowledge; be patient, try to understand and give them information.

9

Controlling messages in the nursery

The subject of this chapter is about some of the ways people use to control other people, in a destructive way, in the nursery. These messages are sometimes quite open and sometimes rather hidden.

Open control

Sometimes people try to control other people quite openly by threats, by force and by moralising. In *controlling communications* the spoken message is, briefly, 'Do this' or 'Don't do that', but the unspoken message is that one person is more important than an another – whether wiser, or simply more powerful than the other.

There are obviously times in nursery work when you have to let people – children, fellow staff, parents – know what is acceptable behaviour or what the rules are, and Chapter 11 will cover how to do this constructively.

The sort of *controlling* messages we are thinking about here are destructive rather than constructive. They include communications when a person is disparaging of another or says things that make them feel small or silly. They sense that the speaker is arrogant, judging them, or moralising about them, trying to control them against their wishes – in short, showing no respect. The feelings aroused can cause *interference* (see page 20), that is the listener blocks out part of the intended message and only hears the part that is hurtful. Statements like:

'I would never have done it like that. Why didn't you ask me first?'
'It's so lazy, leaving everything lying about. Always clear up before the children go out.'
'How can she eat her dinner, when you've filled her up with biscuits?'

'Your problem is that you don't listen.'
'Waste not want not – you should never have thrown it away.'

In all of these the speaker is trying to *control*, by using language and expressions that are likely to hurt, taking no account of the other's feelings. They are all likely to result in interference and are best avoided. Their strongest message is that the speaker disapproves, not that there are better ways of doing something.

'Controlling' messages can be destructive and hurtful

Let us take another example, this time where the control message may seem less obvious. An insensitive worker on a children's ward notices that a mother, changing her baby, is not managing very well. She takes the baby away, with a sigh and says, 'I showed you how to do that this morning!'.

Here, as well as reminding the mother that she had been given a demonstration earlier, the worker 'puts the mother down'. An important part of the message is that the mother is inexperienced – and is rather silly into the bargain. This sort of communication can only be harmful. Firstly, it may damage the mother's self-confidence in looking after her baby. Secondly, it harms the relationship – which should be one of warmth and trust – between the mother and the member of staff. This is disastrous because mothers and the people who take care of their children – whether they are childminders or school nursery nurses, whether they work in a day nursery, a hospital or a playgroup – need to be able to cooperate and to respect one another.

Similarly, communications which are lacking in respect can be destructive between colleagues, between staff and students and, most important of all, between nursery workers and children.

Points to discuss or think about

In the example given above, the message – that the hospital worker thinks she is superior to the mother – is not very hidden, although she could always protest, 'I only told her that I'd shown her this morning. I didn't mean anything else by it'.

(a) Do you remember from your own experience any episodes where someone passed on a message, without actually saying it in so many words, that they were superior to someone else? What happened?

(b) Are there times in nursery work when you need to be especially careful not to communicate in this way?

(c) Which of the following pieces of advice would you give to a new nursery worker (you are only allowed one): 'Try always to be tactful even if you don't feel like it' or, 'Always show respect to people because they're fellow human beings with feelings just like you'?

Observation

During the next few days be on the look-out for anyone trying to control another person – adult or child – by using blaming or moralising language. This could be in real life or on television. What happens?

Hidden messages

Some communications in nursery work contain harmful messages which are much more difficult to spot. Subtly, often unintentionally, they convey the idea that certain groups of people, parents and children, are different from the rest in important ways. Such hidden messages convey that some groups are not valued in the same way as others. The undervalued groups include people from ethnic minority communities compared with the rest, girls compared with boys and people with special needs (such as mentally or physically disabled people) compared with others. One of the results of this discrimination is that the undervalued groups do not have the same chances in life as other people – they do not have equal opportunities.

Equal opportunities

In order to put things right, many groups, including the National Nursery Examination Board, the National Childminder's Association, some local authorities and other employers, have equal opportunity policies. These policies cover many different aspects of equal opportunities, for example, how job advertisements are worded and the sort of records that are kept. These are important areas, which you may care to look into yourself. Here we are considering how communications can contain hidden, controlling messages, which work against equal opportunities in nursery work.

Stereotyping leads to unequal opportunities
Hidden control messages are often contained in *stereotypes*. This happens when we do not see people as individuals, but are more concerned with them as members of a group, for example, an age group, a profession, a racial group, whether they are men or women, boys or girls.

When people use stereotypes they focus on those characteristics which are thought to be common to all members of one group. It can include statements about supposedly good points as well as bad ones. Here are some examples:

'Black children have a natural sense of rhythm.'
'Boys are more daring than girls.'
'All nursery workers are gentle.'
'Black people are better at athletics than whites.'
'A mother's place is in the home.'
'Girls are gentle.'
'Physically handicapped people are cheerful.'

Stereotyping limits how you think about people by concentrating on certain characteristics and not others. Sometimes stereotypes are about 'good' qualities, sometimes about 'bad' ones.

Like other *controlling* messages, stereotyping can be a source of *interference* for the listener, that is, it can block or distort communication (see page 20). Anyone who thinks they are being stereotyped can feel angry and defensive, unprepared to listen.

In addition to this, by stereotyping other people you are more likely to hear them say what you expect to hear – not what is actually said. It is easy to distort what is said to fit in with personal prejudices.

Stereotypes about admirable qualities are as prejudicial as unpleasant ones. If a nursery worker says, 'Black children are so athletic' that is still denying them their essential individuality – some black children are very athletic but others are average, and others not very good. It is a way of lumping people together, ignoring ways in which they are different.

If nursery workers view people according to stereotypes, they are likely to encourage characteristics which fit in with the stereotypes and even excuse undesirable behaviour on their account: children may be moulded into ways of behaving which do not, in the long run, serve their best interests. For example, it is somehow all right for a boy to be rough and a girl to be timid. Or those black children who are not particularly musical or athletic may not feel 'permitted' to do well in other sorts of activities because they do not live up to the initial expectations of the stereotype.

Points to discuss or think about

(a) In your experience, is there much stereotyping to be found in work with children?
(b) Can you think of any other 'positive' stereotypes as well as those already mentioned?

Observation

During the coming week become aware of any stereotyping you come across. It could be in a nursery, on television or elsewhere.

Social control

Stereotypes serve to control people and keep them 'in their place'. But people who use stereotypes may be quite unaware of this; they may not understand that their communications contain hidden messages which exercise power and control over others. But very early in life children come to understand the value that society at large places on different groups of people.

Sexism

Sexism is one example of social control. It is the way in which girls and women are denied some of the opportunities open to boys and men, including the very different messages boys and girls receive from their earliest days. Much research shows how babies are prepared for their role in life according to their sex. From the beginning children come to know something about their social role – and that of other people. Boys as well as girls soon learn what is expected of mothers as much as fathers. People treat even very little babies differently according to their sex. (An example is given in the points to think about and discuss, opposite.) People have different expectations of them, and as they grow older boys and girls continue to be treated differently.

Aspects of organisation may also carry messages. Often girls are asked to line up on one side and boys on the other. In one nursery boys and girls had separate games at the Christmas party. The hidden message to the children in these practices is that differences based on sex are highly important. And so they are, but only in very special and biological contexts – unless we

make them otherwise. Research in schools, including in nursery schools, shows that teachers pay more attention to boys than to girls. Fortunately there is evidence that special training makes teachers more even-handed.*

Other hidden messages may be found in the book corner, with more pictures of boys than girls and of boys playing a more important part than girls. In many nursery books also, there are few pictures of black people.

Exercise

Find a children's book that you think would be popular with four-year-olds. Go through the book and notice the part played by girls and the part played by boys in the first five pictures.

1. Count how many men and boys there are compared with women and girls (if the book is about animals very often it's clear if they are meant to be male or female).

Is a girl or a boy in the foreground of the pictures? Is the person who is drawn biggest a girl or a boy in each picture?

Notice how often male characters are: doing

something; watching someone else do something; helping someone else. What about the female characters?

2. Are there any pictures showing people from ethnic minorities? If there are go through the exercise above, but this time look at the different parts played by black people and white people.

When you've examined your book, decide if it contains any hidden messages about the boys and girls and about people from ethnic minority backgrounds. Would it be a good book to use in the nursery? If other people have done this exercise, compare notes with them.

Points to discuss or think about

1. What do you think are the hidden control messages in the following statements?

> 'Will one of the boys carry the chairs?' (*teacher*)
> 'Big boys don't cry.' (*childminder*)
> 'She's a real little tom-boy!' (*nursery officer*)
> 'Girls on that side, boys over here.' (*teacher*)
> 'We are going to ask if any of the fathers could help put up the stalls and if the mothers could make a cake.' (*head teacher*)
> 'We put boys in blue cots, girls in pink.' (*ward sister*)

*See 'Gender differences in teacher-pupil interactions: a meta-analytic review' in *Research in Education* (Manchester University, 1987)

If children are limited to books with pictures like these then the suggestion is that girls and women provide an audience for boys and men, that boys are active, that black children are athletic, that the family car is for the men in the family while women are usually involved in childcare, and that the normal family is white with two parents

2.   Here are some experiments* carried out with babies:

(a)   Fathers were shown their new-born children for the first time, in a cot, through a glass screen. The scientists running the experiment asked each man, after he had viewed his child, what his impressions were. Those with a little girl baby used typically feminine characteristics to describe her; she was pretty, sweet and so on. The boys' fathers, on the other hand, used much more active and masculine qualities to describe them.

(b)   Many experiments have been carried out in which a baby is dressed 'unisex' and handed over for a few minutes to an adult. Sometimes 'it' is given a girl's name, sometimes a boy's name. On other occasions the adult is left to decide the baby's sex. Always, if the baby is thought to be a little girl, then the adults treat 'her' more gently and soothingly. If the child is thought to be a boy, then 'he' is played with in a more rumbustious manner.

Do you think that these experiments have anything to tell us about how 'feminine' and 'masculine' characteristics arise?

*See 'The eye of the beholder: parents' views on the sex of the new-born' I. Z. Rubin et al in *American Journal of Orthopsychiatry* 44, 1974, and 'Baby X: the effects of gender labels on adult responses to infants' C. Seavey et al in *Sex Roles* 1 (2) 1975

Racism

Racism means all the ways in which black people are treated as less important than other people in our society and therefore put at a disadvantage. This includes direct insults, and even in the nursery children can be heard using racist insults – racist jokes and attacks. But racism also works through less direct means and these get through to children. One four-year-old black child told her mother, 'I don't like very black people'. Other dark-skinned children may fantasise that their skin will turn white.

It needs a conscious effort to avoid racism and promote equal opportunities, and in some nurseries workers have not thought about this. This may result in experiences which are alienating for children and parents alike. This does not happen in a direct way – many nursery workers would be shocked at any suggestion that they treat some children differently to others. But unless staff make a conscious effort, racism – carried in hidden messages – is very difficult to avoid. The next time you go into a playgroup, nursery, children's ward or into a childminder's look out for the following:

— Are there play materials, books and toys to which ethnic minority children and parents can relate?
— What about pictures in books, on walls and in

jigsaw pictures? Can all the children find people to identify with?
— What about dolls?
— Is there brown 'flesh colour' paint as well as pink 'flesh colour'? And brown plasticine?
— Does the dressing-up box have a good collection of clothes for the different children in the nursery, for example, sari lengths, Rasta caps, black wigs and so on?
— Does the home corner have a choice of foods and cooking utensils?
— What about the major festivals celebrated in the local communities? Are there signs that these are celebrated with the children?
— Do 'interest tables' and other displays have pictures and objects that reflect the local community?

The items above are just a few pointers towards good nursery practice and obviously there are other important areas to take into account, for example, staffing policy: whether the nursery makes an effort to recruit and train workers from different backgrounds; what is done to meet the needs of parents who do not speak English, and so on. If what you see reflects the local community, then there are messages for all the children present – not just to those from ethnic minorities. The message is that staff wish to treat all children and parents with respect, to help them to feel at home and welcomed. In this way staff set the atmosphere for children and families.

If you feel that you do not know enough about a particular ethnic group – how they celebrate an important festival, for example – parents themselves can be your best source of advice. Community groups, your Local Education Authority and Social Service advisers can also provide information.

Some nursery workers may object that anti-racism does not matter in their work, because they work with babies. We know, however, that learning about who you are and your social relationship with other people starts at a very early age and it is important that children grow up with a positive self-image and that parents feel at home. So pictures and toys in baby rooms, hospital wards and at childminders' homes should be chosen accordingly.

Other nursery workers may say something like, 'When I look at a child I just don't see its colour, children are children. I'm colour blind!'. This may be true, but a child's colour is an important part of their identity and should be acknowledged in equipment, pictures, toys and activities and other practices!

Points to discuss or think about

You work in an inner city school with children from different ethnic groups. It's Christmas and the teacher decides to put on a Nativity play. She follows her usual practice: all the shepherds are played by boys, all the angels by girls; Mary is white, one of the three kings is black.

Would you have any objections to the play? Why do you answer as you do?

Control: key points

- Many interpersonal communications contain messages about control. Some of these are quite open, such as when one person exercises or tries to exercise power over another by insulting them or moralising about their behaviour or putting them down in some other way.
- These controlling messages can be a source of interference in interpersonal communication because of the distracting emotions they arouse.
- Other messages about control can be more hidden.
- Stereotypes can seek to control whole groups of people by suggesting what behaviour is expected from them.
- The toys, books and activities used in nursery work can be methods of controlling people in various ways. They can suggest the behaviour expected from people – whether black people, white people, able-bodied people, handicapped people, girls or boys. They can also suggest that some groups are less important than others by ignoring them and their experience.

10

Conflict: receiving criticism

Wherever you work, situations are bound to occur where you are directly involved in conflict arising from your work, when the subject matter of your communication will centre on differences or disagreements between yourself and others. There will be times when another person, perhaps your boss, perhaps a parent or an angry child, will be critical of something you have done and will tell you about it. On other occasions, you yourself may be critical of someone's behaviour and decide, for professional reasons, to talk to them about it.

People react differently to such situations depending on the circumstances, on who is involved and on their own particular temperament. But it is important to remember that interpersonal conflict does not necessarily have negative results; it can be a starting point from which people come to understand one another better, take more account of the other's point of view and find constructive solutions to their differences.

This chapter shows you how to make use of what you have learned so far in this book to help you to find a positive way forward when someone *confronts* you about something, that is when they come to you and openly tell you that in some way or other you are causing them a problem. They may do this tactfully or, on the other hand, they may not consider your feelings at all and be, in your eyes, quite offensive.

Nobody likes being criticised, even when the criticism is justified. It can shake your confidence or make you feel upset and angry, especially if the criticism is expressed with hostility and aggression. Nevertheless, there are things you can do in the face of criticism which are constructive, rather than destructive, and which can help to build good relationships in your work.

There are five steps to be taken.

1. Keep cool: avoid escalation

You need to be aware of your own feelings and of those of the other person. You will notice how the other person is feeling mainly through non-verbal signs, how they use their voice, their facial expression and so on (see page 6).

In many situations when a person confronts someone else, there are feelings involved which could complicate matters and make things worse. The person who is confronting may feel aggrieved, but also anxious about voicing a complaint. The person at the receiving end of the complaint may also feel emotions rising. But it is important not to let the situation escalate.

For example, a mother is angry because she thinks a nursery worker has taken her bronchitic child out on a cold, wet morning. She is nervous about approaching the worker and is feeling quite agitated. She summons up her courage and marches determinedly up to the worker and gives her a piece of her mind. The worker's immediate reaction is of panic, followed by anger that the mother should speak to her so 'rudely'.

If the worker allows her own feelings to become involved and shows them to the mother the situation could blow up into something far worse, into a situation containing so much *interference* (see page 20) that neither side would really hear what the other had to say. The nursery worker would not hear the mother's very real anxieties about her child and the mother would not hear the explanation which the worker offered.

In such cases, whether the person criticising you is a concerned parent, angry child or a senior colleague, you need to notice signs of agitation or anger arising in yourself which you may communicate to the other person, causing the emotional temperature to rise. If you feel anxious or angry, a conscious effort to calm down is useful. Some people follow the old custom of literally counting to ten but just telling yourself to keep calm can also help.

A cooling-off period is going to be necessary before these two can start to work things out

If the other person is very upset you may need to make decisions about whether your conversation should happen 'here and now'. Is the baby room a suitable place for talking to a visibly irate parent? Would a 'cooling-off period' help? You may have good reasons to believe that it would be better to postpone the interview. If so, explain that you are taking what they have to say seriously but that you could give the criticism more careful consideration if you could talk about it in a quieter place or at a time when you could give it your full attention. Be specific about finding a time and place which would suit both of you.

Exercise

Find different ways of saying, tactfully, that you would like to put off what looks like becoming a heated discussion until another time.

2. Listen: show you understand

The importance of listening carefully to criticism must be emphasised. Let the other person say what they want to say without interrupting: hear them out. Then let them know that you understand the substance of their criticism by reflecting back what they have said. This is also a way of checking that you understand, because if you have misunderstood they will put you right (see Chapters 5 and 6 on reflecting back).

For example, a colleague comes and says, 'I'm really fed up with the way you always leave the equipment out on a Wednesday afternoon so that I've got to put it away when I come in on a Thursday morning. It's not good enough. I've not got time to do your work as well as my own. Just because you leave early on Wednesdays doesn't mean you can't clear up. I can't clear your things and get my own room ready at the same time.'

A reply that lets your colleague know that you had received the message would be the most helpful. Something like, 'You've always got to clear up my stuff on Thursday and you can't get on with your own work?' which reflects the content of the criticism: they have to tidy up after you. It is possible that they will not realise that you have really heard, at first, and may repeat some of their complaint: 'I've got enough to do on Thursdays, I can hardly manage as it is'. Reflect back again, including reflecting their feelings: 'Because I don't clear up, you feel really pushed on Thursday morning'.

Any solution, explanation or apology you want to give may not be properly heard until the criticiser knows that you can understand their point of view, that you are not avoiding it or denying it; in short you are taking their experience seriously. In facing criticism, as in all nursery work, respecting the other person's experience is important.

3. Apologise

If you are in the wrong, apologise. Everyone makes mistakes, it is just part of everyday life. It could be that you have misunderstood, or forgotten, some instruction; or perhaps you had not realised how your actions would affect another person. The best way forward is to acknowledge that the other person has cause for complaint, say that you are sorry and, if appropriate, what steps you are going to take to put things right. In the example above, you might reply, 'I'm sorry about the equipment, I thought that you'd want to use it, but I should have checked. I'll pack it away in future.'

4. Put right misunderstandings

In some cases all that is necessary is to put right any misunderstanding that underlies the criticism. So in the first example given on page 52 (where the mother is worried about her bronchitic child), having listened carefully, the best thing for the nursery worker to say would be something like: 'You thought Carol went out to play, with her bad cough? I can understand why you're annoyed. But in fact she didn't go out at all, I've kept an eye on her all day'.

5. Win/win situations

If the situation cannot be resolved by a simple explanation or apology, then the most useful attitude in any conflict is that both sides should be satisfied if at all possible – you want the best outcome for everybody. So, when you understand the other person's point of view and the reasonableness of it, reflect this back. Then try to explain your own point of view (the next chapter goes into this in greater detail) and invite the other person to join you in finding a solution that suits both of you – even if there has to be some give and take. If you try to win at the expense of the other person, by putting them down in some way, you may find that both of you (and maybe other adults and children with whom you work) lose out.

For example, Steve, a nursery worker, comes to Nadina, in the next room, and complains that Nadina's group always has musical activities when his group is having a quiet time. At first Nadina is angry because Steve's manner is abrupt. But she keeps calm and listens to Steve's complaint and lets him know that she understands the problem and Steve's feelings about it.

Steve relaxes somewhat and Nadina explains that her group has music at that time because it is their turn to have the tape deck, but she is sorry for the disturbance. She asks Steve if they can think of any solutions between them. They think of all sorts of ways out of the problem, including using different rooms and swapping round the tape deck rota. In the end they come up with an idea that suits both of them, to the benefit of both their groups.

Points to discuss or think about

(a) Can you remember times when having something out with someone – or their having it out with you – seemed to clear the air? What about other occasions when relationships have deteriorated after having it out?

Were there any differences in how matters were handled in these different cases?

(b) Which of the ways of coping with criticism would you find most difficult? Cooling the situation down; listening and showing that you understand the other person; apologising; putting right misunderstandings; finding a win/win solution?

Practice

If any incident arises in which you are criticised use the skills you have learned about in the chapter. Later write notes about it – what happened, how you responded and the outcome.

Role play

There are two parts, Reg the father of Gary, aged two, and Sally his nursery worker. Reg found bite marks on Gary's leg yesterday evening and is very upset. He speaks to Sally about it first thing in the morning.

Try the role play twice; once with Sally being on the defensive and then with her trying to be as constructive as possible, in the ways suggested above.

What differences did you notice in Sally and in Reg in the two approaches?

Receiving criticism: key points

If you find yourself at the receiving end of criticism or complaints at work, the following points can help you to be constructive, to the advantage of everyone concerned.

- If necessary, cool the situation down. Be aware of any interference caused by your own feelings and keep calm. Notice non-verbal communication of feelings coming from the other person.

- Try to see the other person's point of view and let them know that you understand. Reflect back what they say to you. This helps to clarify their complaint and shows that you are treating them with respect.
- Everyone makes mistakes, so apologise if you are in the wrong.

- If there is a misunderstanding, clear it up.
- Avoid a win/lose situation and use all your interpersonal skills to see that you both 'win'. Suggest that both of you think of all the different ways you can to get round the difficulty and together choose the one which is most mutually satisfactory.

11

Conflict: confronting another person

The last chapter was about the times when, at some time in your work, someone has a complaint to make about you and you find yourself at the receiving end of criticism. This chapter is about situations when you feel the need to *confront* another person – adult or child – about their behaviour. You think that you should tell them directly about what is wrong, in order to bring about an improvement. This should only arise for sound, professional reasons. That is when you believe that the other person's actions are not in the best interest of the children, whether directly or indirectly. For example:

— In a playgroup a parent who comes in to help does not get involved with the children; you feel that her own child, and other children, miss out because of this.
— A colleague does something that seems thoughtless, perhaps chatting to other staff when there is a lot to do; this means that the children get less attention.
— You are a childminder. A parent is frequently late picking up his child. You believe that the child becomes anxious when his father does not turn up on time.
— One child is aggressive towards another. You think that this is undesirable for both children.

In all of these cases you have a choice: either to put up with what is troubling you or to do something about it by *confronting* the person involved. *For people who are not experienced in nursery work, and students, it is often better to consult a senior worker about what to do.*

Although keeping quiet has its attractions – and no doubt you can think of cases where this is clearly the best course – there are also occasions when to do nothing would be a mistake and you must take action. For example, you cannot stand by and allow children to hurt one another.

Sometimes people are anxious about confronting, even when they know it is necessary. They bottle up their feelings and their resentment may be shown in other, less direct ways. Eventually, when they can put up with things no longer, they explode and more damage is done than if the problem had been tackled earlier. The other person may understandably feel aggrieved and say words to the effect of, 'Why didn't you tell me before, I didn't know I was causing problems?'.

Points to discuss or think about

(a) Can you think of any situation which has deteriorated because someone does not confront another person about their behaviour?
(b) In your experience are there occasions when it's better not to confront another person about unhelpful behaviour?

How to confront constructively

It is reassuring to realise that confrontation can be handled well, so that no-one is unduly hurt and there is a satisfactory outcome.

Stay calm
Once again, just as when you are on the receiving end of criticism, you need to stay calm in order to be constructive, to choose the right words and the right approach (see page 52). If your feelings are not under control you may say things which undermine relationships and which you will regret later. Also, a display of anger or annoyance on your part can arouse feelings in the other person which *interfere* with how they receive part of your 'message'. They will not really listen to what you have to say because they may be more concerned

with their own anger or anxiety which results from your attack. So remind yourself to stay calm.

Choose the time and place

You have to decide if this is the time and the place for confrontation (see page 53). In the heat of the moment, when you are feeling angry about something, you may not be able to handle a confrontation so that it works out well. If a child, who has just hit another, is now throwing a tantrum, it is better to weather the storm and wait for him to calm down before taking any further action. Similarly, a time when an adult is obviously distressed about something may not be a good time for confrontation.

Check misunderstandings

Once you have decided to confront, the first step is to check, politely and sincerely, that there is no misunderstanding on your part or that of the other person. This gives you the opportunity to back down gracefully, if the mistake is your own, and the other person the chance to apologise if the mistake is theirs. For example:

NURSERY NURSE: Excuse me, did you know I'd just cut all that paper to take for Rainbow Room?
TEACHER: Oh, I'm sorry, I thought it was for us.

Or you could check whether you understand the situation properly:

NURSERY NURSE: Why did you throw all the toys out of the home corner and on to the floor?
CHILD: Because there was a fire and they all jumped out.

NURSERY OFFICER: Have I got it right, I thought you said Mary was going to help me on Fridays, but she thinks she should be in Sunshine Room?
OFFICER-IN-CHARGE: I'm so sorry, I'd forgotten to tell her.
Or: No, if you remember that was for after Easter, when the new assistant comes.

Of course, the non-verbal communication must back up the verbal communication; an accusing tone of voice could make the same words carry a very different meaning. Imagine the effect of, 'Excuse me, did you know I'd just cut all that paper to take for Rainbow Room?' snarled between clenched teeth!

Being tactful

Confrontation needs tact and sensitive handling, but some situations call for special care. Such a case is the example given previously of the playgroup mother who does not get at all involved with the children. You should check if she understands what she should be doing at the playgroup – it could be that she thinks she is there only to keep an eye on the children. Such a discussion would need some introduction, perhaps about how she is enjoying being a helper or if there are any difficulties, rather than a bald question, 'How do you think you should be spending your time here?'. Possibly she feels shy and you need to help her find her feet by encouraging, rather than by confronting.

Exercise

You could do this in twos or as a whole group. Imagine that you are the person who is doing the confronting in each of the examples below. Find other, more effective ways of confronting. Suggest other ways of opening the conversation, checking if there is any misunderstanding on the part of the other person, or any difficulty that you do not know about.

1. Ward sister to nursery nurse who is late for the fourth time in succession: 'You're very unpunctual!'
2. Nursery nurse to an NNEB student who is chatting in the staff room about some sensitive personal details disclosed to her by a child's mother: 'You're not supposed to gossip like that.'
3. Nursery officer to a colleague who has opened a letter addressed to her: 'You've been reading my private correspondence!'
4. Nursery officer to domestic: 'You've not done round the window sills.'
5. Nursery officer to student, putting toys away: 'That's really untidy.'
6. One nursery officer to another: 'You've had our transistor for two weeks now. It's not fair.'
7. Nursery officer to mother who comes late to pick up the children: 'It's really inconsiderate, coming late like this.'

8. Student to four-year-old Gary, who did not hang up his coat: 'You're really lazy today.'

Do not blame

If there are no misunderstandings, and if the other person does not back down, then the next step is to help them understand your point of view better.

Do not blame them, or moralise, or comment on their character – it stops people from listening and from seeing any other point of view (see pages 46 and 47). Also, it does not show respect for the other person. Similarly, do not let your non-verbal communication convey blame. If you say, 'Michael, you're a naughty, spiteful little boy to bite Wayne', perhaps the strongest message Michael gets is that you do not approve of him, while it would be more appropriate to lead him to understand that Wayne has feelings and that Wayne is hurt.

Not using blaming language is vital, but it may not come naturally. Many of us are accustomed to situations where blame and criticism are used in order to control, or attempt to control, others (see below). Perhaps you can remember times when you have been at the receiving end and how you felt about it.

Points to discuss or think about

In the episode below, see how many examples you can spot of moralising and blaming. What effect is it having on Yusef?

Jean, the Deputy Officer-in-Charge, is just about coping today. The Officer-in-Charge is on leave and both nursery officers from the baby room have phoned in to say that they are sick. Jean is the only nursery officer present who has any real experience looking after babies so she decides to cover the baby room herself, with Yusef, a newly appointed member of staff, from another room.

She is called to the phone about an emergency admission. Before she goes, she asks Yusef to wash the bottle just used by the youngest baby and to bring the play-pen and toys back in from the garden – it looks as though it is going to rain.

Jean is away longer than she had hoped. She returns to find that Yusef has not washed the bottle nor brought the things in from the garden. As she thought, the rain is starting to fall. The food for the older babies will arrive in a minute, but nothing is ready. Yusef is just sitting there with one baby on his knee and one crawling on the mat in front of him. The others are in their cots. The following conversation takes place.

JEAN: Look, Yusef, you've not done anything I asked you to. I expected you to get on so we'd be ready for the dinners when I got back. Instead I find you sitting there playing with the babies. You're just not pulling your weight.

YUSEF: I thought . . . I mean I couldn't do everything and Donna was crying and I thought I was supposed to . . .

JEAN: I asked you to do something and you just took no notice. You haven't even washed the bottle out. It's not good enough, you're supposed to be a trained nursery worker – I'd have been better off with a first-year student.

YUSEF: (*sulkily*)   I couldn't find the bottle brush and Donna started to cry so I picked her up . . .

JEAN: Look, here's the bottle brush, under your nose. Now for goodness' sake get on with it and try to get things ready by the time I come back.

'I' and 'you' language

There are ways of avoiding blaming and criticising. If you need to confront another person get into the habit of telling them how their actions affect you and your work (including your responsibilities towards parents and children) rather than how awful, inconsiderate, untidy – or whatever – they are. This is using 'I' language, not 'you' language; the emphasis is on you and on problems that arise for you as a result of the other's actions.

One social skills expert suggests a useful formula for talking about how the other person's actions affect you: 'When you . . . I feel . . .'. For example:

> 'When you talk to staff from the other room I feel really rushed trying to get everything done.'

Not:

> 'It's really inconsiderate leaving me to do all the work because you want to chat.'

The first approach gives the other person information she might not have had before, that her actions put pressure on you, and may in itself be enough to bring about a change. It could also be an opportunity for her to tell you about her reason for talking to colleagues – and you might find the reasons acceptable.*

Setting boundaries

Sometimes a confrontation is necessary because of your professional responsibilities towards the people you work with and concerning rules at work. These rules are often referred to as boundaries and they can affect adults and children.

Boundary setting: children

You sometimes need to tell children about boundaries, about what is acceptable and what is not. If one child hits another you separate them and say to the aggressor, 'We don't hit other people – it hurts'. In this way you protect one child and give the other a clear understanding of what is expected. This makes for security, children know where they stand. You are also giving a reason for the rule and one which helps the child to remember that other people have feelings too. At an earlier stage, when a baby or toddler does not understand language very well, then a firm 'No', accompanied by removing them from the scene of the 'crime' sets the boundaries of acceptable behaviour.

Points to discuss or think about

(a) 'I think you should tell children off if they do something wrong like hurt someone else or take their things. You should tell them that they're naughty'. What do you think of this opinion?
(b) Is there any difference between a nursery worker telling a child off and a mother doing it?

Boundary setting: adults

Here is an example of a confrontation with an adult which involves setting boundaries.

You are in charge of a childminders' drop-in centre; a new minder smokes while she is looking after the children – and local authority policy is against this. Clearly it is your responsibility to see

*See *A Handbook of Communication Skills* Owen Hargie (Ed.) (Croom Helm, 1986), pages 413–4 for a discussion of 'I' and 'you' statements in confrontation.

that this does not happen. In the first place you should check that she knows about the rule and make the boundaries clear: 'Did you know we've got a no-smoking rule when the children are here?'. This gives her information which she might not already have; it also gives her the chance to back down gracefully.

If she persists you need to tell her where you stand and what your responsibilities are (using 'I' language): 'I have to see that the no-smoking policy is carried out', 'I feel that it's best not to smoke in front of children because of the example', or, 'It worries me when I see toddlers near lighted cigarettes'.

It is a good thing to show that you understand her point of view and the effects this rule is going to have for her. For example, you could say that you are sorry for any consequences of your action: 'I'm sorry you're missing your cigarette'.

But it is not helpful to apologise for asking her to keep to the rules – that's part of your job. 'I'm sorry I've got to ask you to stop smoking' is just not appropriate, in fact it may not even be sincere.

Think of solutions: problem-solving

As we saw earlier (page 54), when there is conflict try to be creative, find ways out that satisfy both sides – 'win/win' solutions – and involve the other person in finding them. In the example above the minder could go into the next room for a cigarette while you played with the children – if both of you thought the children would be happy and you did not have conflicting duties.

When you are problem-solving you may need to suggest several ideas before you find something mutually acceptable.

Problem-solving with children

It is also possible to use problem-solving with children once they are old enough to understand. If a child is acting against the interests of other people, point out that the behaviour is not permitted; that is, set the boundaries (see above) and briefly give the reason. Then ask for the child's reason:

'Why are you hitting Tracey?'
'She's got my car and I want it.'

Next involve the child in suggesting other ways of obtaining the required result: 'What else could you have done to get your car back?'. Children soon get used to this approach and come up with ideas for themselves. You are helping them to be creative, also they are learning that there are socially acceptable ways of solving their own problems.

Role play

You may be able to think of times when you wanted to confront someone but were nervous of doing so. Choose one such occasion for a role play. Do it twice, the first time ignoring the advice given in this chapter. The second time handle the confrontation as constructively as possible.

How did it feel, each time, from the point of view of the confronter and the confronted? What did the onlookers notice?

Exercises

Practise confronting so that you feel that you can do it effectively should the occasion arise. In twos confront one another about the following situations. Each take a turn at both parts. After each confrontation talk about how you both felt – was it a successful confrontation from your point of view?

1. A mother confronts a childminder because her child was not properly wrapped up to go out on a cold day.
2. A nursery worker confronts a mother who continually forgets to bring back clothing – pants and tights – lent when the child wets herself at nursery. The nursery is short of spares.
3. A nursery worker confronts another worker about always taking too long a coffee break.

Observations

During the next week or so observe confrontations as they occur around you – for example in a nursery, a shop or on television. Include confrontations between adults and between adults and children. How do both parties react? Are the confrontations handled well?

Check what happens against the 'key points', given below.

Confronting another person: key points

- Sometimes it is professionally necessary to confront other people, adults and children, about their behaviour. That is, if someone is acting in such a way against the children's interests, either directly or otherwise, then you should speak to them about it and ask them to change.
- When you confront, stay calm in order to avoid *interference* (see page 52).
- Choose the best time and place for confrontation. This may be here and now, or it may be better to delay the confrontation.
- Do not use the sort of language, or tone of voice, that sounds like blame or telling off.
- Check if there is any misunderstanding which has brought about the behaviour.
- Say how the other person's behaviour affects you, or people for whom you are professionally responsible.
- Tell them about *boundaries*.
- If at all possible, *problem-solve* with the person you have confronted, that is, work creatively for solutions. With children this is a way of showing them that socially acceptable solutions are possible.

12

Confidentiality

Although this is the last chapter in the book to deal with a specific aspect of interpersonal communication, it is not the least important. It covers some of the issues of confidentiality that you are likely to meet as a nursery worker. This chapter is about how you treat information which is *disclosed* to you (see page 37), and whether you pass it on to any one else or not. It does not cover subjects like how sensitive information is stored or who has access to written records. These are important but they are matters of policy which may differ from one place of work to the next.

Private information can be passed on to you in different ways, here are some of them.

Parents confide in you

In the course of your work, especially if you get on well with people, you will find that parents confide in you and tell you about their worries and problems. This may come about because they like you and find you trustworthy, which is quite likely if you treat them with sensitivity and respect. But, quite apart from their feelings about you, they may also need to confide in you just because of the job you do. Sometimes they will tell you family details so that you can understand their child better.

For example, you tell a father, when he comes to pick up his toddler, that she is not her usual self; she is being a bit whiney and clinging. He explains that her mother is suffering from depression and has been taken into hospital. He did not tell you earlier because, he says, 'People can be funny about mental illness'.

This father would of course expect you to treat what he has told you as confidential; he has let you know because you work with his child, and would not have told you otherwise.

Senior staff pass on private information

As well as parents disclosing confidential matters, senior staff may also pass on private information about families – not because it is interesting but so that you can do your job properly.

For example, Daren's father is separated from the family and there is a court order forbidding him access to Daren. The nursery head teacher passes on this information to all staff who are in contact with Daren. This is necessary because of the risk that his father might turn up at school and staff might, unsuspectingly, hand Daren over to him.

Being trustworthy

When someone, parent or colleague, discloses private information about children and families, obviously you do not gossip about it. It takes little imagination to understand how hurtful it would be for your own private business to be discussed by other people. In everyday life some people find it exciting to receive private information and to be able to pass it on and see the effect it has on others. But nursery workers should think of themselves as professionals, who do not divulge information that should be kept confidential. If you have a need to discuss confidential information at work you should go to a senior staff member:

— in hospital a nursery nurse would go to the ward sister;
— an officer-in-charge of a day nursery would go to their manager; a nursery officer would go to the officer-in-charge;
— in school, confide in the head teacher;
— a playgroup worker or a childminder would go to the social service colleague with whom they usually liaise.

This is not the same as gossiping.

Points to discuss or think about

Do you think that it is all right for nursery workers to discuss private information about families in the following circumstances: in case conferences; at home; over coffee in the staff-room; in staff meetings; in discussions during training courses? Can you think of any exceptions to the answers you have given?

Being responsible

Sometimes it is necessary to pass on confidential information for the sake of the child – just as the head teacher in the example above told staff about the separation and court order. Senior nursery workers are likely to meet this more often than juniors but it is something that all nursery workers should be prepared for: a parent will confide in you and you will have to think whether to keep what they say to yourself or to pass it on.

What are the ground rules for deciding when to pass on information about a child, or a family, to other colleagues?

'Need to know'

Decisions about passing on information should be made on the basis of whether other staff *need to know*.

— Is it necessary to tell colleagues so that they are better able to look after the child, or to offer a better service to the family?
— Are there dangers for the child or the family if this information is not passed on to other members of staff?

Who needs to know

If the answer to either question is 'Yes', then the information should be passed on to all those who need it professionally. If you are in a junior position then it should be passed on to whoever is in charge, who will then decide if it should go any further. If you are ever given information by a parent that worries you or upsets you it is your duty to discuss it, in confidence, with your boss.

Some day nurseries have a system of 'key workers' by which one person is especially responsible for liaising with one family and is seen as the person who *needs to know* the relevant information about the family. In other nurseries all staff who ever work directly with the child are given necessary information. This could include all staff who cover (act as substitutes) for people who usually work with the child. Decisions about this are made by senior staff.

For example, Linda's parents have divorced and her father has not been allowed access to Linda. Linda's mother tells the officer-in-charge of the day nursery that in no circumstances is Linda to be allowed to leave the nursery with her father. The officer-in-charge lets all staff know about this because it is possible that any of them could be in charge of Linda, at some time during the year.

Dangers in passing on information

As well as advantages, there are also dangers in passing on information. These include, first and foremost, *infringing the privacy of the family concerned*. It cannot be stated too strongly or too often that families have a right to privacy and infringing it should only happen in the real interests of the child.

Secondly, there is no reason why staff should be burdened with unnecessary details about the families they work with. Some nurseries and family centres only take children whose families are in extremely difficult circumstances – but knowing all the details of the children's backgrounds would be of little help to the nursery workers concerned.

For example, Cathie is on the non-accidental injury register. The local authority social service department believes that in the past her parents have beaten her. So they offer the family a place for Cathie in a day nursery where they expect the staff to be alert to any signs of injury.

Clearly it is necessary for staff to know that Cathie is on the register so that they do not lightly dismiss any bruising, or other damage. But there is no need for them to know other family details which could distress them or even prejudice their relationship with the family.

So if a mother confides in you about her own spectacularly unhappy childhood, there is no need for you to pass that information on. It has nothing to do with how you look after her child and no danger will arise because other staff do not know about it. But, once again, if you find that a confidence is upsetting or worrying, you should tell your boss about it. Nursery workers should be able to look to whoever is in charge for professional support, so that they can do their work without undue stress.

Declare you are going to pass on information

If you decide that what you have been told should be made known to others, then you should say so to the person who has confided in you.

For example, Deidre is a mother at the nursery; you get on well with her. She tells you that her sister's children, also at the nursery, are left alone for hours every night while their mother is working at a local pub. She has often heard them crying as she passes the house. She knows that there is a paraffin heater in the bedroom. She has spoken to her sister about it but her sister says that there is nothing she can do – the family needs the money. Deidre says, 'Please don't say anything, I don't want to cause trouble, but I'm worried sick about it.'

This is an awkward position for you to be in and a type of situation which could arise for childminders, special needs staff and playgroup workers, as well. On the one hand you believe that there is real danger for the children, on the other you feel loyalty towards Deidre who has confided in you.

In a situation like this, where it seems likely that children are at risk, you have no option but to pass the information on to whoever is in charge of the nursery. But *you must tell the person who has confided in you that you are going to do so*, otherwise they are in a false position. They may believe that you are relating to them in a purely personal way, as a friend, while for you professional responsibilities towards the children have priority. One way forward is to suggest that it would be better for the other person to take the information further themselves. If they are unwilling to do this, you can say that you know it is very difficult for them but that, for the sake of the children, you are going to tell your boss, for example the head teacher or the officer-in-charge, about it. If you are working as a childminder or in a playgroup, the person to inform would be the social worker who carries out the registration procedures in your local Social Services Department.

Points to discuss or think about

Read the following cases (overleaf) and, if possible with a partner or in small groups, decide what you would do. Read over the 'key points' which follow to help you to come to your answer. There may not be one 'right' answer; you may think of different circumstances which would affect what you would do. For example, in Case 1 Saleem's mother may have brought him to the nursery that morning.

Gossiping is unprofessional; it does not respect people's right to keep personal matters private

Case 1

Saleem is a three-year-old at nursery school. One day, when you are looking at his painting, he says, 'My mum shouted at my dad and she's gone away now'. How do you react? Do you report it to anyone or not? Should you, or a senior worker, 'check out' if what Saleem says is true? What are your reasons for your course of action?

Case 2

In a maternity unit a weeping mother is having problems feeding her new baby. She tells you that she suffered severe depression after the birth of her first baby. What do you do, if anything, about this information? Why?

Case 3

You are an officer-in-charge of a day nursery. Gary's mother tells you that his father has AIDS. To whom – if anyone – do you pass this information on? On what grounds do you make this decision?

Case 4

You do a home visit to a family where the child has just started nursery class. Wayne's mother tells you, in confidence, that his father is beating him. What do you say to her and what action, if any, do you take?

Confidentiality: key points

- Nursery workers are often given private information about the children and families they work with.
- This information should not be talked about to other parents, nor to anyone who is not professionally concerned with the child or the family.
- Information should be passed on to other colleagues if they *need to know* for the child's sake.
- Passing on information infringes the privacy of the people concerned. It can also be a burden for colleagues and one which, in some cases, prejudices staff against a parent. Passing on information should only be done if really necessary.
- If you have any worries about information you have received, you should pass it on to a senior worker who will then take responsibility for whoever else, if anyone, should know.
- If you decide that you are going to talk to a senior colleague about a parent's private affairs, you must let the parent know you are going to do this, as part of your professional duty.
- Some employers have their own policy about confidentiality. For example an education authority may have a policy about AIDS or about the non-accidental injury register. A senior colleague can let you know what this is.

13

Interpersonal communication: overview

This last chapter takes an overview of what you have read in the rest of the book and picks out some of the main themes and ideas.

In nursery work effective interpersonal communications are those which, directly or indirectly, serve the needs of the children. All nursery work is for the sake of the children in your care. They come first and you use your professional skills and knowledge for their benefit. This includes your practical skills, like being able to prepare a bottle or look after a grazed knee, as well as your knowledge of subjects such as child development. Your interpersonal skills and your knowledge of social interaction are also used first and foremost for the sake of the children. It may be that the children are affected indirectly, for example, when you listen and respond acceptingly to an anxious parent, or settle a conflict with a colleague in a constructive way. In such situations making good use of your interpersonal skills has a beneficial effect which can indirectly affect the children. You can also be directly beneficial in your face-to-face interactions with children. You can use your skills to:

— listen and observe carefully;
— avoid interference;
— reflect back;
— use questions with discrimination;
— confront about undesirable behaviour without blaming.

This will encourage children to communicate to the best of their ability and so can help them to develop their own powers of communication.

Effective communicators can take the other person's point of view. To understand how someone else feels about something you have to listen carefully to what they say and observe their non-verbal communications. If you are alert to the various signs and messages the other person sends, you can make better judgements about how to respond to them. So, for example, you spot when someone is upset and take that into account in what you say (or decide not to say) and how you say it.

This is true of work with babies, as well as with adults and older children. With babies you need to be sensitive to how they are feeling – sleepy, alert or crying – and to the various cues they send you about their enjoyment of your games and talk together: often you take the lead from them. You know when they are ready for you to take your 'turn' to play more and to time your contribution so that it fits in.

Effective communicators are aware of the part that feelings play in interpersonal communications. Your own and other people's feelings play a large part in interpersonal communications. If you are aware of another person's feelings you can understand their 'messages' more completely. If you are more aware of your own feelings, you are less likely to let them *interfere* with communication.

Effective communicators respect other people. Taking into account the other person's point of view and letting them know that you do so, whether by your actions or words, is one way of showing your respect for the babies, children and adults you work with. You do so when you reflect back the content of what they say and, sometimes, the feelings they express verbally, or in other ways. You acknowledge their experience, you do not dismiss or ignore it.

You try to work professionally with all the people you come into contact with. There may be some people – adults or children – whom you do not like as much as others; but nevertheless you try to communicate with them with respect and take your share of responsibility for how you get on together. You find ways out of conflict which meet their needs as well as your own; you do not use blaming or judgemental language in order to try to control them.

Similarly, in a spirit of respect for people, you avoid stereotypes and other messages which control some children to their disadvantage. In this way you promote equal opportunities for members of ethnic minorities, for black children and their families, for children who are disabled and for both girls and boys.

If people trust you with personal information you respect their right to privacy by not gossiping about it. You only pass it on if you think it is necessary for the sake of a child and you tell your informant that you are going to do so.

In conclusion

Interpersonal communication is going to play an important part in your working life. The skills introduced in this book are ones which you can improve and develop throughout your working life. They are skills which will be of service to the parents whose children you care for, to the colleagues who share your work, and above all to the many children whose physical, emotional and intellectual well-being will, to some extent, be in your hands.

Suggestions for further reading and other resources

Social Work with Black Children and Their Families Shama Amed et al (Eds) (Batsford, 1986)

Person to Person Michael Argyle and Peter Trower (Harper and Row, London, 1979)

Special Times – Listening to Children Philip Carr-Gomme, Rachel Pinney and Meg Robinson (Children's Hours Trust, London, 1985)

A Guide to Anti-Racist Childcare Practice Nicole Celestin (Volcuf, 77 Holloway Road, London N7, 1986). Also from Volcuf an exhibition: *Unequal and Under Five.*

Race and Social Work V. Coombe and A. Little (Tavistock Press, 1986)

There's a Good Girl: Gender Stereotyping in the First Three Years of Life – a Diary Marianne Grabrucker (The Women's Press, 1988)

Explaining Death to Children Earl A. Grollman (Ed) (Beacon Press, Boston, 1969)

Children and Race Ten Years On David Milner (Ward Lock Educational, 1983)

Practical Counselling and Helping Skills Richard Nelson-Jones (Cassell, 1988)

Human Relationship Skills Richard Nelson-Jones (Cassell, 1987)

Body Language Alan Pease (Sheldon Press, London, 1981)

Baby Play Pat Petrie (Century Hutchinson, London, 1987)

Infancy: World of the Newborn Martin Richards (Harper and Row, London, 1980)

The Child's Entry into a Social World R. Schaffer (Academic Press, 1984)

Young Children Learning Barbara Tizard and Martin Hughes (Fontana, 1984)

Working with Under-fives David Wood, Lynet McMahon and Yvonne Clanstoun (Grant McIntyre, 1980)

Building Blocks Early Years Education Project The Rampway, Castlemead Estate, Camberwell Road, London, SE5. Materials for multicultural education.

Index